100 DAYS WITH THE HOLY SPIRIT

A DEVOTIONAL FOR
LOVING INTIMACY
WITH JESUS

100 DAYS WITH THE

HOLY SPIRIT

MICHAEL KOULIANOS

 All emphasis within Scripture quotations is the author's own. Take note that the name satan and related names are not capitalized. We choose not to acknowledge him, even to the point of violating grammatical rules.

DESTINY IMAGE® PUBLISHERS, INC.
P.O. Box 310, Shippensburg, PA 17257-0310
"Promoting Inspired Lives."

This book and all other Destiny Image and Destiny Image Fiction books are available at Christian bookstores and distributors worldwide.

For more information on foreign distributors, call 717-532-3040.
Reach us on the Internet: www.destinyimage.com.

ISBN 13 TP: 978-0-7684-6454-2
ISBN 13 eBook: 978-0-7684-6455-9
ISBN 13 HC: 978-0-7684-6474-0
ISBN 13 LP: 978-0-7684-6456-6

For Worldwide Distribution, Printed in the U.S.A.
1 2 3 4 5 6 7 8 / 28 27 26 25 24

He doesn't choose golden vessels. He doesn't choose silver vessels. He chooses willing vessels.

—Kathryn Kuhlman

CONTENTS

1

Consumed with the Beauty of Jesus

There is not enough room in the universe to list all that the Holy Spirit does. He is the power that keeps what we know as life intact. He is the air we breathe and the literal energy of the Godhead. I believe that we will have a glimpse into His amazing role and power when we are in Heaven. The appreciation will continue to unfold in hearts for thousands upon thousands of years. On top of this, He is a real person with feelings and desires.

However, God's will is that we see His greatness while we are here on earth. As great and awesome as the Holy Spirit is, He does have a passion that is above any other. He may communicate on many levels and in different ways. He whispers to some and shakes others. To some He speaks through an ocean and to others through the beauty of a desert sunrise. Some enjoy a prayer closet while others see Him on every tree and in every breeze. One thing is certain: Within the various methods, tones, and scenes through which the Holy Spirit speaks, He really only says one thing...JESUS.

The Holy Spirit is absolutely consumed with the beauty of Jesus. He thinks Jesus is just amazing. Now, this does not mean that He is less in nature or deity than Jesus. Absolutely not! Rather, the Holy Spirit's focus on Jesus lets us into the very heartbeat of the Holy Spirit and, for that matter, the nature of the entire Trinity. The Father, Son, and Holy Spirit are always pointing us to another member of the Godhead. This quality is so beautiful and highlights an aspect of God that I believe is far too often overlooked in the Church today—the humility of God. When is the last time you heard a teaching on humility in a Sunday morning church service, on television, or on social media? Humility is not just something humans (should) have. It is perfectly portrayed and seen in the character of God.

It looks like this: The Holy Spirit points us to Jesus. Jesus points us to and perfectly represents the Father. The Father, in turn, says, *"This is, My beloved Son"* (see Matt. 3:17; 17:5; Mark 9:7; Luke 9:35). The Holy Spirit is the One who makes it possible to hear the Father and see the Son. And the beautiful cycle continues forever and forever. Yes, the Trinity is beautifully captured by one another. As I say around the world to thousands and thousands of people, "The Trinity is not a board of directors in Heaven, trying their best to fix the world's problems. No! They love one another deeply and are in covenant. It is their deepest joy to reveal each member of the Trinity to us."

You are unlike any other, Holy Spirit. I long to hear You, to see the ways You're moving, and to learn from Your character. I want to fall even more in love with Jesus, today. Help me to go even deeper into Your presence so that I can see His glory in a new way. Give me a glimpse of the beauty of the Trinity through Your eyes! Lord, show me Jesus.

2

HE QUALIFIES THE CALLED

On paper, according to natural ability, I am the least qualified to preach the Gospel. As a great person once said, "He does not call the qualified; He qualifies the called." What is the qualification from Heaven's point of view? You got it. It's plain and simple: Have you been filled and clothed with the Holy Spirit? I believe that had I "earned" the ministry with natural ability, I would be tempted to point to myself in times of success.

I am well aware of the fact that the boy who shook under the power of God for hours on the Orlando Christian Center floor was completely unlikely to succeed in the ministry according to the world's standards. What the world does not understand is that the Holy Spirit loves taking the unlikely and giving them His power instead of our own. This way, He is forever glorified. Today, as I stand on platforms and see the crowds, I know one thing for certain: It's all Him. He has done great things. I often say, "Jesus, thanks for the privilege. You are everything." Now more than ever, I believe the following verse: *"'It is not by might. It is not by power. It is by My Spirit,' says the Lord of hosts."* (see Zech. 4:6).

So today, I stand on the shoulders of those who have paid a price. I am praying for God's grace to carry on the power of the Spirit to a generation who often chooses natural gifting over a surrendered life. The world needs you to yield your life to God. Jesus is waiting to take your weaknesses and use them as trophies for His glory. When the Holy Spirit comes on you, you will become a different man or woman, just like King Saul did. That which frightened you, you will attack. Your limitation will dissolve into springboards that catapult you into your destiny. Mountains of fear will flatten before the Holy Spirit's touch on your life. At the end of the day: When you get Him, you get everything. You need nothing but God because every other need is found in Him. This is your moment. This is your time.

Thank You, Holy Spirit, that my life is no longer in my own hands. Thank You that fulfilling my destiny doesn't depend on my ability or self-sufficiency. I bring to You my few loaves and fishes—all that I have—and I lay them before You. I trust You completely. My life is Yours. What is the next step You are calling me to?

3

God Almighty

I had a healing service scheduled at a church. A few hundred people gathered, and we began to worship the Lord. The presence of God was beautiful. Once I felt the Lord's presence saturate the meeting, I began to preach. I learned to do that. I learned to wait until He's real to me to start preaching. You see, when He's real to us, we actually have something to talk about because we're leading people to a person who we're experiencing in the moment.

But something happened in that meeting that we had never experienced before. After the preaching, we began to worship the Lord again. Many were saved, and it was a time of celebration. During the worship, a physical wind blew from the right side of the pulpit and began to fill the room. I will never forget what happened. People began to scream, they began to cry, they began to shout and laugh, and I knew that I knew that the Lord was healing people.

One girl had entered the service wearing a back brace, and when the Holy Spirit blew through that room, her back began to audibly pop. She physically felt her back realign, and her mother heard her back pop back in place. So, the girl tore her brace off and came to the platform to testify. I'll never forget that moment as long as I live. Two other girls were called forward to the platform. They were set free and filled with the Holy Spirit. It was like He came and worked so quickly that we could not keep up with what He was doing.

You see, when He comes, you know it. I've heard some people say, "Well, I think the Holy Spirit's working in my life. I think He's working in my ministry." If there's one thing I can promise you, it's this: When He does, you know He's there. When He's working, you know He's working. When He touches your life, you'll never be the same. If He's really moving, if He's really come, there will be no doubt in your mind that He's there. Let's remember that He is God Almighty.

In Your presence, there is healing. It is who You are. You are the restorer of all things broken, always leaving me stronger than before. I bring every broken piece of myself to You today. Holy Spirit, I need You. Fill me with Your presence. Bring to mind one person that You want to touch today. How can I partner with You to see restoration come to another's life?

4

He Fills the Room

He loves to make a statement. Do you remember that when Solomon finished the temple, there were 120 priests sounding trumpets? Second Chronicles 5:13–14 says that "*...the house of the Lord...was filled with a cloud, so that the priests could not continue ministering because of the cloud; for the glory of the Lord filled the house of God.*" When He comes and fills a room, He makes our job much easier. I used to know (or thought I knew) so much. I used to know what songs to sing and when to sing them. I would pray for anything that moved. I tried this, and I tried that. Then the Holy Spirit told me, "If you'll just create the setting and the atmosphere where I am welcome, I'll come and do the work." And you know what? He has, and He has never quit doing the work.

It happened again in the upper room. Do you remember the 120 that were gathered in Acts 2?

> *When the Day of Pentecost had fully come, they were all with one accord in one place. And suddenly there came a sound from Heaven, as of a rushing mighty wind, and it filled the whole house where they were sitting. Then there appeared to them divided tongues, as of fire, and one sat upon each of them. And they were all filled with the Holy Spirit and began to speak with other tongues, as the Spirit gave them utterance* (Acts 2:1–4).

This was a fulfillment of the promise from Joel 2:28–29: "*…I will pour out My Spirit on all flesh; your sons and your daughters shall prophesy. Your old men shall dream dreams, your young men shall see visions. And also on My menservants and on My maidservants, I will pour out My Spirit in those days.*" He is the King of a mighty entrance. Just think tongues of fire, a thunderous wind—this is a demonstration of power. He came to earth in an incredible manner.

> *I will spend my life getting to know You, Holy Spirit. I will devote myself to becoming one who walks closely with You. I welcome You to come in any way You want. Your presence is Heaven, and I am so grateful that You have given me complete access. What do You want to reveal about Your nature, Your heart for me, and Your heart for the world?*

5

Passionate about Jesus

As I said earlier, the Holy Spirit has one job: to reveal Jesus to us. Jesus said, *"He will testify of Me"* (John 15:26). That means the Holy Spirit wants to have a conversation with you and you can bet that it's going to be about Jesus! I'm often asked, "Michael, what's your fixation with Jesus all about? Don't you think you talk about Him too much? Maybe you should change the subject, man. There is more to the Christian life than Jesus." My response as to why I am so into Jesus is simple: it's because I've been touched by the Holy Spirit.

You see, Jesus said, "*...out of the abundance of the heart the mouth speaks*" (Matt. 12:34). In a nutshell, that verse means that whatever is in your heart will eventually come out of your mouth. You will speak what's on the inside of you. Some talk about money non-stop, and others about politics, because politics and love of money flow through their hearts. Some talk about church all the time because the desire to have a big church fills the corridors of their hearts. Well, the Holy Spirit speaks of Jesus because Jesus is on His heart. And when the Holy Spirit comes to live in my heart and I yield to His passion and voice, His passion becomes my passion. His voice marries my voice. What He says, I say. Or should I say, Who He says is Who I say.

So, if you're wondering whether or not you have been rocked by the Holy Spirit, the barometer is very simple: Are you crazy about Jesus? I'll never forget the tender whisper of the Spirit in 2009 at our little apartment in Orlando, Florida. There I was, waiting on the Lord, and the Holy Spirit spoke these words to me: "Michael, if the people in your meetings leave with a greater understanding of your ministry than they do of Jesus, it's proof that I have not led the meeting." WOW! What a statement. I began to connect with and understand the passion of the Holy Spirit and His feelings. He is passionate about Jesus. He is doing His job, which is to point our hearts to the beautiful face of the Son of God, gladly on the earth.

You are the greatest gift of my life, Holy Spirit. You open up my understanding of God's Word, You show me the heart of Jesus, and You fill me with Your presence. I will never take Your praise out of my mouth. I will never be ashamed of my abandoned love for Jesus. What aspect of Jesus' nature would You have me dwell on today, Holy Spirit?

6

Revealing God's Ways

Why such a focus on the simplicity of Jesus Christ? Why doesn't the Holy Spirit just bypass Jesus and point us directly to the Father? Can't He just tell us about Himself the entire time? The answer is simple: a man can only know God through the God-Man. God's nature and ways are beyond our reach as humans unless we see Him in the Son.

God basically said, "Look, I'm going to make this so simple for you now. My grace and love are causing Me to come to earth and wrap Myself in a body. I will literally be seen, heard, felt, touched, and followed. I am going to reveal myself to you as the perfect and visible will of God with a body. You will never ask this question again: 'What is God like?' Simply look at Jesus." Never again do we have to wonder about the ways of God.

If you are confused about God's perspective on sickness and healing, look at Jesus. If you are wondering about God's desire to provide for you, look at Jesus. Is God merciful? Look at Jesus. Is God bold? Look at Jesus. Should we pray? Look at Jesus. The point is simple: Jesus is perfect doctrine and our literal life source and model (see John 1). On top of these amazing truths, He holds all things together, and *"in Him all things consist"* (Col. 1:17). So, when the Holy Spirit points you to Jesus, He is pointing you to the Answer to your every need.

You have made a way for me to know You, the God of the Universe. I will spend the rest of my days wrapping my mind and heart around that gift. Thank You for showing me God's heart in a way that I could comprehend. Thank You for not being a distant God. Thank You that You want to be known by me. I will fix my eyes on Jesus every day, trusting that all answers are found in Him.

7

For the Sake of the Father

Beyond the Holy Spirit's motive to save you with a revelation of the One He loves, Jesus, it is also for the Father's sake that He does so. Perhaps you've never seen His ministry from this angle. Have you ever stopped to think about the incredible price that the Father paid as He offered up His only Son for a world that hated Him? Yes, Jesus paid the ultimate price, but so did the Father. He watched His Son get tortured and mocked. He offered Jesus to those who tied Him to a post and stripped Him naked before tearing His precious back open with the Roman whip, a whip covered in sharp bones for the tearing of flesh and lead balls for deep bruising.

Imagine the heart of the Father as sinners assaulted His precious Son. A songwriter refers to Jesus as the "Darling of Heaven." I love that because it paints a beautiful picture of Jesus' value from Heaven's perspective and, more importantly, from the Father's perspective. Not to mention that it was by the Father's design that His Son suffered. Jesus prayed, "If there is another way, let this cup pass from Me" (see Matt. 26:39). Clearly, if there was another way, the Father would have chosen it, but this was His perfect will—that Jesus die the death of the cross and be tortured brutally. Again, the Bible says, "It pleased the Lord to crush Him" (Isa. 53:10).

This is a price that we cannot imagine. The Father offered His Son to the world willingly and watched Him get tortured so that you and I would belong to Him forever. I will never forget holding my son Theo up as I played with him. He was under one year old, and he used to love it when I held him up high. There we were, in our small apartment in Orange County, California. There was a small hallway outside the guest bedroom, and that is where I was playing with Theo. As I held him up high, I had an internal vision of the crucifixion. Holding my son over my head, I clearly heard the Lord say, "I gave My Son to be lifted up on the cross and to die. Could you give yours?" My spirit responded, "No! No way! I could never do that." The Lord said, "I gave My Son. I even gave Him for My enemies." Wow. The revelation of love that pierced me came wrapped in a picture of the price that the Father paid. I pray the Holy Spirit will open your eyes to see that the Father paid the ultimate price when Jesus died.

Well, what does that have to do with the work and heart of the Holy Spirit? What does the price the Father paid have to do with the Holy Spirit's obsession with Jesus? It's quite simple: He is bringing the Father a reward for the price He paid when He sacrificed His beloved Son. The reward is a people who love His Son forever and who will be the eternal children of the Father. The Father sowed His Son, and the Holy Spirit is glorifying Jesus so that the Father will receive His harvest...you and me.

Father, help me to never turn away from the suffering of the cross. Holy Spirit, give me a new revelation of the price that was paid so that I might stand before the Father with love and thanksgiving. Help me feel the depth of love that is at the root of that sacrifice. Let my life bring You glory forever!

8

He Covers

The Holy Spirit is not new to the scene. In fact, He's been around since the very beginning of time. We know that He is completely God and has been in existence forever. He is not bound to time; time lives in Him.

We read about this in Genesis chapter 1. The Scripture says, "*...the Spirit of God was hovering over the face of the waters. Then God said, 'Let there be light'; and there was light*" (Gen. 1:2–3). That's right, the Holy Spirit has been moving and touching and revealing God on the earth since day one. He still hovers today.

The Hebrew word for *hover* carries the sense of an eagle hovering over its nest, protecting it while it waits for its eggs to hatch. This is what the Holy Spirit does today. He hovers over the water of our hearts. After all, the Scripture says that *"deep calleth unto deep...all thy waves and thy billows are gone over me"* (Ps. 42:7 KJV). Our hearts and our spirits are like deep wells of living water, and the Holy Spirit hovers over that deep. Before we're born again, our spirits are dead. Just as darkness covered the face of the deep on the earth in Genesis chapter 1, darkness covered our innermost being before we met Jesus. And so, the Holy Spirit begins to hover over our darkness, over our sin, over our blindness, and He slowly begins to touch us.

He is the master at changing the atmosphere over our lives and our hearts. When He comes on the scene, He begins to moisten the soil of our lives. He starts to bring a tenderness to our hearts. This prepares our hearts for God to speak.

Thank You, Holy Spirit. Because of You I am alive. I have met Jesus and am born again, a new creation. Today, I consciously open my heart and soul to You all over again. Would You prepare the soil of my heart for all that You know is coming? Would You soften any place that has become hardened in me? I want to be fertile ground for the move of God.

9

He Prepares Our Hearts

I'm sure we all heard wonderful sermons before the Lord touched us. Perhaps we even heard the Gospel message preached clearly, but many of us continued in the life of sin even after hearing great preaching. What made the difference that moment we came to Jesus? What was it that finally caused the same message to stick and change us forever? It was the presence of the Holy Spirit. It was His loving hand breaking up our hardness, our stubbornness, and making our heart moist, giving the Gospel just enough room to take root in all of us. He is the master evangelist.

The Bible says in Genesis chapter 2, verse 6: *"a mist went up from the earth and watered the whole face of the ground"* (Gen. 2:6). This is a beautiful picture of what took place in the Garden of Eden. That mist is a prophetic symbol of the presence of the Holy

Spirit in our own lives. It is God's desire that our hearts become a Garden of Eden. It is God's desire that we never dwell in a dry land. The Scriptures tell us that the rebellious live in dry land (see Ps. 68:6).

The Holy Spirit is the Spirit of rain, the Spirit of moisture, the Spirit of fruit, the Spirit of color, and beauty, and growth. And this is what He brings our way. Once the atmosphere is prepped and He has done His work in us, He carries the power of the Gospel, which is the Word of God, into our lives. Just as light came upon the darkness in Genesis chapter 1, the light goes on in us. We can see. We're no longer blind. The face of Jesus rests before us. He becomes more real to us than anything or anyone. This is the beautiful work of the Holy Spirit.

> *I will pursue You, Holy Spirit. I will run to wherever You are moving, just to be close to You. Show me if there is anything in my heart that would hinder Your presence. I give You complete access—I lay down my dignity, my control, and my expectations. Have Your way in my heart. Fill me with Your vision for my life.*

10

THE BREATH OF GOD

Genesis 2:7 says, "*And the Lord God formed man of the dust of the ground, and breathed in his nostrils the breath of life; and man became a living being.*" God took mud and perfectly formed you and me. The Father is so meticulous. The Son is so precious and faithful. The Father willed our creation, and the Son administrated it. God perfectly put us together. The Bible says that He formed man of the dust of the ground by putting man in His own hand. Imagine the detail of the human body. Just think of the perfection that God has given us in our bodies. Our eyes, our veins, and our brain are more complex than any computer. Consider the way He's shaped us and designed us to keep disease away from us, the beauty around us that we're able to experience because of our five senses—all of this because the Lord formed us with beauty. The Bible says, "*I am fearfully and wonderfully made*" (Ps. 139:14).

However, even though God formed Adam with such incredible and perfect detail, Adam was still dead. His beauty did not guarantee him life. In fact, he lay absolutely lifeless while being perfectly and wonderfully made. It was not until God breathed the breath of His life into the nostrils of Adam did Adam come to life. Does this sound familiar to you? Does this sound like much of the Church in the West? Beautifully designed buildings, chairs designed to keep you awake and keep you comfortable during a service. I'm making a point, and the point is this: Structures, programs, money, construction, and crowds do not guarantee that God has breathed His Spirit into our lives.

If I were to paint a picture for you of what it looks like to be religious, it would be exactly what I am talking about right now: form with no power, structure with no cloud, speech with no breath. In fact, the Bible says in the last days that many would have a form of godliness but deny the power (see 2 Tim. 3:5). Let's look at our own lives. Is most of our time spent focusing on the details of what we construct on our own? Or is it spent obtaining and enjoying the breath of God?

Every part of me was made to know Your presence. I was designed—spirit, soul, and body–to be attuned to Your movements. Holy Spirit, heighten my perception. Remove anything from my life that is dulling my awareness of You. I come to You with no agenda. Help me to become aware of Your presence in this moment.

11

Born Again

Have you ever wondered why the Lord breathed into Adam's nostrils? It's because to receive this breath, Adam had to be face to face with God. We must remember that at this point, Adam was dead. Adam could do nothing to receive the breath of God but lie there dead. This is a beautiful truth that I pray many, many more in our generation will understand—that as we lay there lifeless, losing our own will and dying to self, God begins the dance. It is God who draws near to us first, who breathes into us.

What could Adam do before he was alive? Nothing but just lie there. Today, the very fact that you're reading this book is proof that God has touched your life. Can you picture Adam lying there in the hand of the Lord after being formed and the Father so lovingly bending down and coming face to face with Adam? God literally breathed the Holy Spirit straight into his nostrils. This is what it means to come face to face with God.

Once Adam received that breath into his nostrils, he would breathe it out of his mouth. The first experience in Adam's life was to breathe out the breath of God, to release what he had received. This is true worship. This is true life in the Spirit. Once Adam's eyes opened, his first sight would be the face of Jesus Himself. Jesus is the face of the Father. Second Corinthians 4:6 says that *"...the glory of God...is seen in the face of Jesus"* (2 Cor. 4:6 NLT). Only the Holy Spirit can open our eyes. Only the Holy Spirit can cause us to breathe. Only the Holy Spirit gives us the breath of worship. Only the Holy Spirit gives us vision to see the face of Jesus. I have been in meetings while ministering when the Holy Spirit's presence was so thick and tangible that it seemed I could literally breathe in His Presence. He is the air we breathe.

Now you know why Jesus breathed on His disciples when they were born again and He said, *"Receive the Holy Spirit"* (John 20:22). This tells us that the Son of God can sit right in front of you, but unless the Holy Spirit indwells, you cannot be a child of God. I'm so glad that the Father, the Son, and the Holy Spirit work together so beautifully in our hearts.

> *Thank You, Lord, that You have always pursued connection with me. Thank You that, even when I was dead in sin, You chose me and drew me close to You. Holy Spirit, I need Your life-giving breath to fill me today. I want to receive Your presence so that I can release all that You are into the world around me.*

12

He Roams the Earth

He also sent out from himself a dove, to see if the waters had receded from the face of the ground. But the dove found no resting place for the sole of her foot, and she returned into the ark to him, for the waters were on the face of the whole earth. So he put out his hand and took her, and drew her into the ark to himself. And he waited yet another seven days, and again he sent the dove out from the ark. Then the dove came to him in the evening, and behold, a freshly plucked olive leaf was in her mouth; and Noah knew that the waters had receded from the earth. So he waited yet another seven days and sent out the dove, which did not return again to him anymore (Genesis 8:8–12).

We all grew up hearing this story of Noah. I remember as a little boy being amazed at the number of animals, the size of the boat, and the incredible amount of rain and water that flooded the earth. As I began to read the Scriptures with a prayerful heart and more consistently, I discovered that as amazing as Noah's accomplishments in construction were, this story is not about a boat. As incredible as the amount of animals that found their way onto the boat is, this story is not about corralling a large number of animals. As incredible as the amount of water that covered the earth in that time is, this story is not about rain in the natural. Neither is the part about the dove flying away really about releasing a bird. That dove is the Holy Spirit. That ark is Jesus Himself. The window out of which the dove flew is the side of Jesus that was pierced on the cross. Those waters symbolize two things: the judgment of the world and the waters of baptism, both killing the old man.

Why did Noah wait seven days to send out the dove? Because it's on the eighth day that new life is promised. Seven means perfection, and eight signifies a new day. What was the job of the dove? The job of the dove was to let Noah know what the status was outside of the ark. And so the Holy Spirit roams the earth today, communing with the Father and the Son, sharing His feelings about what is happening in our world. Why an olive branch? It's because it's a picture of peace and a picture of the Anointed One who would be crushed in Gethsemane in a garden of olive trees—the One who would ultimately become our Peace. No, the Holy Spirit is not new to the scene. He's always been there.

Holy Spirit, You have always been here and will always be. You usher in peace and are one with Jesus and the Father. Show me the areas of my heart where You see growth and fruit. I want to know You deeply.

13

Searching for the Bride

Remember, all of the Scriptures point to Jesus, according to John chapter 5 and Luke chapter 24 (see John 5:39; Luke 24:27). So let's have a look at the beautiful types and shadows of Jesus in Genesis chapter 24. Abraham is the Father. Isaac is the Son. The faithful and oldest servant of the house is the Holy Spirit. The father has a desire to find a bride for Isaac just as our Heavenly Father wants His Son, Jesus, to receive the reward of the Church, which is a wife and a bride.

The servant, the Holy Spirit, is the One whose job on earth is to find a bride for Jesus. Notice verse 3 says, "*...you will not take a wife for my son from the daughters of the Canaanites, among whom I dwell*" (Gen. 24:3). In other words, the Father does not want, or will not allow, His Son to be married to those who follow the ways of the world. The Holy Spirit will not offer union in marriage to Jesus for those who do not want Jesus. Can you picture the Holy Spirit moving throughout the Church as He prepares and looks for a bride for Jesus, the One He loves?

Finally, the servant found Rebekah in verse 15 while he was sitting on a well (see Gen. 24:15). Can you see it? The Holy Spirit and the Well. The Holy Spirit and the Well are always together. The Holy Spirit is always resting on the revelation of the Well of God, Jesus Himself. And so, the future bride, Rebekah, came to the well. Jesus only marries those who come to Him and want His water and the life that flows from Him.

You are so intimately involved in my life, Holy Spirit. You hear the Father's heart for me so clearly, and You are so eager to help me hear His voice also. I want to be called one who loves Jesus above all else. Prepare my heart for those moments, like Rebekah, beside the well. I want to offer my King everything I have.

14

He Adorns Us

The Bible describes when Abraham's servant first saw Rachel: "*Now the young woman was very beautiful to behold, a virgin; no man had known her. And she went down to the well, filled her pitcher, and came up. And the servant ran to meet her and said, 'Please let me drink a little water from your pitcher'*" (Gen. 24:16–17). Did you know that the Holy Spirit sees you as being beautiful? And if you've given your heart to Jesus and live a life in His presence, you are a pure virgin in His sight. I love that the Scripture says: "*no man had known her*" (Gen. 24:16). This is a picture of being separate from the world, not tainted with the ways and concepts of the system of the world. Freedom from sin as a lifestyle.

The gifts of God—verse 22: "*So it was, when the camels had finished drinking, that the man took a golden nose ring weighing half a shekel, and two bracelets for her wrists weighing ten shekels of gold"* (Gen. 24:22). Gold speaks of divinity in the Scriptures, the nature of God. The nose ring symbolizes that the Bride belongs to Jesus. The bracelets on the wrist indicate that our work and our hands belong to Jesus. But these gifts also speak of the gifts of the Holy Spirit. It is the Holy Spirit who gives these gifts, just as the servant gave these gifts to Rebekah.

Verse 43 says, *"Behold, I stand by the well of water; and it shall come to pass when the virgin comes out to draw water, and I say to her, 'Please give me a little water from your pitcher to drink'"* (Gen. 24:43). Remember, the Holy Spirit is looking for virgins who love the Well, Jesus Himself.

> *I sit in joyful anticipation, Holy Spirit, eagerly waiting to see how You are going to move in my life during this season. You fill me with peace, regardless of the circumstances, and I delight in Your presence. I choose praise, today. I will abandon myself in worship, Holy Spirit. Will You fill me with Your power and love?*

15

All About Christ

How complicated some people have made the Christian life! Shouldn't the Christian life be about Christ? I mean, after all, if He does not come, what do we have? Shouldn't church be about the One who purchased the Church? Shouldn't reading our Bible be about the One whom the Bible is about and the One who inspired it? Shouldn't worship be about the One we're worshiping? And shouldn't prayer be about the One to whom we're talking? It was at that moment I realized that simplicity needed to flood our hearts again.

Do you remember when you met the Lord? That moment when He became real to you? You didn't have theology or a Christian education, but you did have Jesus and you realized, "He's all I really need." You felt His presence, the presence of the Spirit, and instantly, His reality became everything to you.

For many, Christianity is about everything but the Person. It's about dos and don'ts. It's about weekly attendance in church. It's about a specific devotional time. While all of these are good and beneficial—in fact, I highly recommend them—without the person of the Lord, Christianity is dead. In fact, without Him, there is no Christianity.

If Jesus is not actually in the room by the Holy Spirit when we gather, we are not having Christian meetings. You may as well join a country club or some secret society because it is His presence—and His presence alone—that makes anything we do "Christian." The Christian life is the life of Jesus in us and through us by the Holy Spirit.

Strip away anything in my life that has made my walk with You more complicated, Holy Spirit. It's all about You, Jesus! Holy Spirit, would You show me any area of my life that has become more complicated than necessary?

16

THE WAYS OF THE SPIRIT

I remember when I was backslidden and away from the Lord, certain sins gripped me. I struggled in my mind. I struggled in my ways. I fought and fought to be holy. I remember walking into church feeling guilty and ashamed week after week. My parents pastored a church. My dad would ask me to get up and pray, and I felt like garbage because I was bound with sin.

When a temptation would come, I would wrestle against it and rebuke it. I would bind and loose. Oh, I had mastered what I thought was spiritual warfare, only to find out that the temptation would grow stronger and stronger, even when I warred against it. This is when I realized that whether I was fighting it or submitting to it, giving the struggle attention was fueling it. So, to simply war against it was only making it stronger.

Then I began to experience the presence of the Lord. This was the game changer. All of a sudden, He would come my way, and the Holy Spirit would brush my heart and pull on the strings of my desire. I would give Him my attention. I would talk to Him, speak to Him, and worship Him, and He would distract me with His beauty. His presence became so overwhelming that I forgot about my struggles. As we tend to the presence of the Lord, our struggles die on their own.

Ezekiel 36:26–27 says, *"I will give you a new heart and put a new spirit within you; I will take the heart of stone out of your flesh and give you a heart of flesh. I will put My Spirit within you and cause you to walk in My statutes, and you will keep My judgments and do them."*

How many of us fight to keep the laws of God but lose these wars day after day because we don't understand the ways of the Spirit? Following the Spirit, who is within us, causes us to walk in the laws of God. That is the beauty of the New Covenant. We call this the "law of life in the Spirit." As you yield to the Holy Spirit, you join the life of Jesus, and Jesus Himself has fulfilled the law. Maybe you ask, "Michael, how can I be free from sin?" It's very simple: Give your heart and your attention to Jesus the next time the Holy Spirit asks you to. This is not an excuse to disobey the Scriptures; rather, it is the secret to obeying the Scriptures by simply looking to the Lord.

So, what is the plan of God pertaining to your freedom? He will put His Spirit in us, and because His Spirit is in us, He will cause obedience to flow from within us, which is our deepest place, and this makes it simple to be an obedient child. There is a key to freedom that I would love to share with you, and it is this: True freedom is a Person, and your victory comes through His victory.

When you fellowship with the person of the Lord, you connect with the victory of the Lord. His life becomes your life, and your life becomes His.

> *My struggles are real, but Your presence is even more real. I don't want to waste my attention on what the enemy is doing. I want to turn my affection and focus onto You alone. Holy Spirit, I yield to You again today. I give my heart over to You completely.*

17

SONSHIP

It's so vital to know who we are in the Lord, but it is much more vital to know the Lord. Today, there is a great move in grace/identity teaching. Let me first say that the grace of God is incredible and absolutely needed. At the end of the day, we all realize that what we have is because of the grace of God. None of us found the Lord. He found us. And none of us accomplish anything in Him without His power and quickening, which is His grace.

We are sons and daughters of Jesus. There is no doubt about this if we've accepted the Lord. However, it is vital we understand that our focus is not to be on who we are in the Lord; it is to be on the Lord. The goal is to experience who we are in the Lord by gazing upon the Lord. We will never become who we are destined to be by focusing on who we are or who we are destined to be. We become who we are to be by looking at Jesus. The point is to become more like Jesus, not more like me, and to do that I must look at Him and Him alone.

The Bible teaches that we become what we worship. As the Scripture says, "They looked unto Him, and their faces were radiant" (see Ps. 34:5). That radiance speaks of the light and the fire of God. In other words, it's the face of God that our face becomes like as we look at Him. We must remember that while we are sons and daughters, we experience true sonship by being led of the Holy Spirit.

I don't want to spend more time thinking about myself than I do thinking about You, Jesus. I want to gaze into Your face, come close to You, and follow Your every move. I want to know You, Holy Spirit. I want to focus on the beauty of Jesus until I become indistinguishable from Him.

18

Led by the Spirit

The Scripture says, *"As many as are led by the Spirit of God, these are sons of God"* (Rom. 8:14). To be led by the Spirit we must look to the Spirit because we can only be led by that which is in front of us.

We are not called to focus on our sonship above the Son of God. My children know that I'm their father, yet they do not have to walk around the house saying, "I am Michael's son. I am Michael's son. I am Michael's daughter. I am Michael's daughter." No, they simply know that I am their father and that I am near them. That in itself gives them assurance that they are children of mine.

If Jesus is in our heart, we will speak of Him. If we are empowered by the Holy Spirit, we will naturally declare the One whom He loves, Jesus Himself. So, you will get much further in your identity in the Lord by understanding something—that as wonderful as our life in the Lord is, no matter how great we become, He is much greater than we will ever be. Even in Heaven when we have been glorified with Him, Jesus will not be bowing down to us and worshiping us, regardless of how wonderful we have become.

We will forever worship Him, and Jesus will always be greater than we could ever be. Make your focus Him alone. Join the obsession of the Holy Spirit and gaze at Jesus.

I know that I am Yours and that You are near me. Help me to experience Your closeness, Holy Spirit. I am amazed by Your holiness, Your righteousness, and Your splendor. I want to be led in every moment by Your presence. Help me to grow in my sensitivity to Your guidance. I am Yours.

19

He Is the Lord

"Now *the Lord is the Spirit; and where the Spirit of the Lord is, there is liberty. But we all, with unveiled face, beholding as in a mirror the glory of the Lord, are being transformed into the same image from glory to glory, just as by the Spirit of the Lord*" (2 Cor. 3:17–18).

What do these verses mean? I've heard it said many times that they mean, "Well, the Spirit of the Lord is here. I'm free to do whatever I want." That's not what these verses are saying. God is telling us, number one, the Lord is that Spirit. That Spirit, the Holy Spirit, is not *any* spirit. He is the Lord.

Number two: The Holy Spirit is not less than the Father and the Son. He is the Lord. Number three: There is a purpose of the presence of this Spirit—to bring liberty. Number four: The purpose of the liberty is to see the Lord as in a mirror. This is beautiful.

This tells us that as we look at the Lord by the Spirit, His face permeates our face, changing our lives and our countenance into the image of Jesus.

Holy Spirit, help me to never minimize Your presence. I never want to speak of You in a way that forgets who You are. You are the Lord. And, because of You, I am able to stop hiding, experience true freedom, and be truly transformed. Invade every area of my life, Holy Spirit. I invite You to change every part of me.

20

Eyes of Fire

I've met many people who are powerful and anointed servants of God. I've met people who have shaken nations for decades. I've met dozens and dozens of leaders whom God has used greatly, but there have been a few who have been a cut above the rest. There have been a few who have marked me.

I must say, the ones who marked me did not mark me with photos of large crowds. The fact that they were famous did not change me. The ones who marked me were the ones who had something intangible about them. It was undeniable. Even with their flaws it was unmistakable. Their faces were different. Their eyes were different. It was as though at times you were looking into the face of the Lord. It seemed like their countenance, their disposition, literally became a container for the character of God.

Some of these people you've never heard of, and possibly you never will, but one thing I can assure you: they will be champions in Heaven. Their reward will not be fame and television time. It will be proximity to the throne of the Father forever. It will be a crown of glorious presence that rests upon them in the ages to come. These people had eyes of fire. These people had joy and brokenness wrapped into their countenance. These people were as bold as a lion but supple as a lamb. They're hungry but content, needy but able to enjoy His presence. This cannot be faked. Whether on a platform or at home, the Lord's Presence seems to rest upon their face. This is true success. This is what the Holy Spirit does. This is what it means to become like the Lord.

I need You, Holy Spirit, more than I've needed anything else. I want to position myself in Your presence. I want to be marked by You and forever changed. Transform me. Teach me what it means to become a place where Your countenance can dwell. I want to be intertwined with You, authentically altered by Your power and grace.

21

The Reality of Heaven

But he, being full of the Holy Spirit, gazed into heaven and saw the glory of God, and Jesus standing at the right hand of God, and said, "Look! I see the heavens opened and the Son of Man standing at the right hand of God!" Then they cried out with a loud voice, stopped their ears, and ran at him with one accord; and they cast him out of the city and stoned him. And the witnesses laid down their clothes at the feet of a young man named Saul. And they stoned Stephen as he was calling on God and saying, "Lord Jesus, receive my spirit." Then he knelt down and cried out with a loud voice, "Lord, do not charge them with this sin." And when he had said this, he fell asleep (Acts 7:55–60).

The Scripture says, "*He, being full of the Holy Spirit, gazed into heaven*" (Acts 7:55), and when Stephen was done preaching and rebuking Israel, the Bible says that his face shone like an angel (see Acts 6:15). Do you know why? It's because he gazed into Heaven.

One thing happens when you're full of the Spirit: Heaven becomes more real to you than anything around you. That's why just before he breathed his last, Stephen said, *"I see...the Son of Man standing at the right hand of God!"* (Acts 7:56). When the Holy Spirit overwhelms us and fills us, our first vision is of Jesus. Our heavenly home becomes our greatest reality until He changes our physical body. Think of how Moses became after being with the Lord. Do you remember that his face began to shine? Why? Because his face took on the nature of that which he was looking at (see Exod. 34:35).

> *So many of my daily worries have grown larger than my awareness of Your presence. Help me, Holy Spirit, to see things as they are. Heaven is more real than anything in front of me. Your presence is my ultimate reality. I want to keep my eyes locked on You. I want my face to shine from Your glory.*

22

I Have Been with Jesus

The disciples were uneducated men who preached boldly. What did the Pharisees say about them? "They knew they had been with Jesus" (see Acts 4:13). Why do you think the Pharisees knew they had been with Jesus? Was it merely because of the content of their speech? I'm sure that was part of it, but there was something more.

Their words were spoken in a certain way. There was a certain tone to their words that was unmistakable. You see, when the Holy Spirit begins to change your life, God changes the filter and the topic. The filter is the heart. The topic is Jesus. When Jesus is preached with a purified heart, it just sounds different, and this is what the Pharisees noticed in those disciples. This is what the world is looking for: people who speak words in such a way that even those who are enemies of God say, "These men have been with Jesus."

To simplify things, drown out all the noise. Eliminate everything from the Christian life that has nothing to do with Jesus. Make it simple again. Begin to speak to the Holy Spirit, and ask Him to speak to you. If you don't hear anything, just wait a little longer. And if you still don't hear anything, then just wait another day. When you read your Bible, just talk to the Lord. Ask Him questions when you don't understand something. The Scripture says, "If we draw near to Him, He draws near to us" (see James 4:8). Simple dialogue with the Lord is what He's looking for. After all, He is your Friend.

I open up my heart to You all over again in this moment, Holy Spirit. Show me any areas that I've been guarding from Your transformation. Reveal to me the parts of my heart that You want to touch today. I lay myself down. I want to be transformed by You. I want the world to be able to say that I have been with Jesus.

23

HEALING POWER

"My words are spirit, and they are life" (see John 6:63). There is an incredible truth hidden in this passage. When Jesus speaks, He actually speaks a language that is the Holy Spirit. So, picture it this way: When Jesus opens His mouth, the Holy Spirit is released as He speaks. When Jesus sent forth His word to heal the centurion's servant, the Holy Spirit began to move to bring immediate healing.

I'm often asked why I believe that it is God's will to heal. While I could debate it theologically, I've learned that doing so really doesn't take us very far. It is much better to demonstrate the power of God to heal than to argue with someone. But there is a portion of the Scriptures that reveals His will to heal very, very clearly. Do you remember when Jesus came into Peter's house and saw Peter's mother-in-law?

Interestingly enough, He simply touched her hand, and the fever left her. Remember, Jesus told us to *"lay hands on the sick, and they will recover"* (Mark 16:18). Is there something special about our hands in the natural? These are the same hands that make breakfast. They're the same hands that pick up our children. They're the same hands that start our car. What is it about our hands or the hands of Jesus that are so vital? It's not the hands themselves. Those are merely the tools that God uses. No, it's the power that flows through them. And here, Jesus simply touches Peter's mother-in-law, and the woman is healed immediately.

To Jesus, even a fever must bow its knee to His power and authority. That tells me that God is interested in the most horrible sicknesses and also in a mere fever. The reason is that the same price was paid to heal a fever and to raise the dead. It was the life and blood of Jesus. So today, you may have a cold, or you may have cancer. Know this: Jesus wants to heal you.

The same Holy Spirit that was released from Jesus to heal the centurion's servant lives within me. Your healing presence has taken up residence inside of me. Thank You, Jesus! I come to You today, certain of Your care and concern for my physical body. Thank You that You care about every fever. Thank You that every sickness—no matter how big or small—must bow to Your authority.

24

OUT OF THE BOX

Healings are signs and wonders, but there are certain miracles that take place that are not limited to physical healing alone. Jesus walked in this power during His earthly ministry.

It's interesting that His first miracle was turning water into wine. Some people ask, "Why would He do that?" While I believe there are prophetic pictures and truths hidden in that passage that reveal the nature of God, we have to give God the right to do things simply because He wants to do them. I'm sure there were sick people at the wedding that day. Some might say, "Why would Jesus waste His time turning water into wine when there were people suffering?" The reason is…because He is Jesus and He can do things how He wants, when He wants, and for whom He wants.

This is a beautiful example of the Lord performing signs and wonders to get our attention.

To be honest, I have seen many signs and wonders in my life that are outside the boundaries of physical healing. I have literally smelled the fragrance of the presence of Jesus in our meetings. Others have smelled a beautiful scent of frankincense similar to what is in the Orthodox and Catholic services. Some might say, "What's the point?" Well, the point is a deeper awareness of the presence of God. I believe that the more we give our attention to God, the more tangible His presence becomes. In fact, the Scripture teaches, "*As* [a man] *thinketh in his heart, so he is*" (Prov. 23:7 KJV). Our lives become what and whom we meditate on.

Forgive me, Holy Spirit, for any time I've limited my expectation of how You can move in my life. I want to throw away all of my own restrictive thinking and, instead, welcome You fully and completely as You are. I am throwing away this box I keep trying to put You in, and I am opening up my heart with anticipation. I want to see Your hand on my life. I want to know You more.

25

A Life of Intimacy

When Adam walked in the cool of the day in the Garden of Eden with the Lord, it was literal. That's right, he actually walked with God. He could see God; God could see him. He spoke to God; God spoke to him. He heard God, and God heard him. He felt God, and God felt him. This is a beautiful, holy life of intimacy that Adam walked in with Jesus. Today, you and I have been invited into this intimacy by the blood of Jesus.

Somewhere along the way, some people began to view God as a concept instead of a person. I absolutely love reading the Scriptures. You will find a significant amount of Scripture in this book. I love my Bible. It is special to me. It has notes in it from people I love. I've wept while reading it, and I chew on the Word of God and feast on it every single day. But if we do not meet the Person to whom the Scriptures point, then the Bible is nothing more than a book to us.

The Holy Spirit leads us to the Scriptures to reveal Jesus. He does not lead us to the Scriptures to reveal the Bible. My prayer is that God's presence would become more literal to you than you've ever dreamed or known could be possible. He is absolutely real—an actual person who longs to reveal Himself to us. He has a will, emotions, plans, and desires. There are things He loves, and things He hates. Some of what we do attracts Him. Some of what we do repels Him. He laughs. He cries. He judges. He forgives. He invites us into a literal, constant walk with Him. The more we walk with Him, the more our world becomes His. This is a very, very deep place in God. This is a place where He actually begins to break into our physical world and lives.

Do you remember when Jesus went up the mountain to pray during His transfiguration? The Bible says that He began to shine like the sun (see Matt. 17:2). His physical body began to take on the properties of His glory. Instantly, a cloud hovered over Him, and the voice of the Father came from the cloud. These are signs and wonders.

Time and time again, the life of Jesus showed us signs and wonders. Today, the Holy Spirit is still passionate about pointing us to Jesus through signs and wonders.

I want to walk with You, God, just like Adam did. I want to become familiar with Your preferences. Thank You that You've made this possible. Lead me into greater intimacy with You. Will You show me one thing, today, that I don't yet know about You?

26

ALWAYS MORE

In 2003, I became the assistant to my father-in-law. These were incredible times of impartation and mentoring that I treasure dearly. I remember being in the crusades and seeing thousands of people healed miraculously. As I began to step out in faith, I began to see people healed when I prayed for them in those meetings.

In 2005, Jessica and I became the pastors of a local church in Orange County. When I began to pray for the sick in our church services, I rarely saw anyone healed, yet when I prayed for the sick in the crusades, many were healed. This was a very difficult season for me. The Lord showed me that as I came into agreement in the crusades for miracles, miracles were taking place under the umbrella of the anointing that God had given my father-in-law. However, in my meetings, there were very few healings. I learned very quickly that if the people coming to our services were going to be set free, as Jesus promised, that I needed my own encounter with God.

I was baptized in the Spirit in 1989, but I personally believe that God has more than one baptism in the Spirit for us, so that for every level in God that we pursue, an actual experience with Him is required to thrust us into that place. So, I began to fast and pray. I began to go after God. I began to seek Him for hours each day. I came to the place where I told the Lord, "If You don't show up in this ministry the way You did in the Scriptures, what's the point of me even being in the ministry? The world doesn't need another gifted speaker. The Church doesn't need more organized meetings. We ultimately need You, Lord. I need You, and if You don't come, I just don't want to do this anymore."

One night in worship, as I closed my eyes, everything disappeared. My surroundings in the natural meant nothing. My challenges vanished. My worries were long gone, my aspirations dead. It was as though the power of God collided with my frail body. I felt a cool breeze go over me like a blanket. My heart began to race so quickly that you could see it beating out of my chest. My hands were bright red, and they were throbbing too. It actually felt like my heart had descended into my hands. I began to drip sweat. I began to cry. I felt like laughing but instead kept crying. I held on to the pew in front of me so that I could stay on my feet.

I knew this was the deeper baptism that D. L. Moody talked about. I knew this was what the Bible spoke of in the Book of Acts when it described the Church being filled and filled again to the degree that the place they prayed in was shaken (see Acts 4:31). This was after the day of Pentecost. God is not interested in just touching us once. God wants us to live in a constant baptism in the Holy Spirit.

> *Holy Spirit, I need a fresh touch from You today. I want to know Your touch upon me. I am so grateful for all that You have given me, for all that You have shown me, but I am hungry for more! I want to live my life in absolute dependence on You. I need to be filled daily with Your presence.*

27

The Word of God

As a boy, I served in the altar at the Greek Orthodox church. It was a big deal in our family and culture to be an altar boy. We had to prepare ourselves and eventually be ordained. One thing that stood out to me was the huge Bible that lay on the altar of communion. It was massive, very heavy. The cover was made of silver and gold. There were precious jewels embedded in the cover. Also embedded in the cover were small paintings of the Lord. To this day I still have never seen a Bible like that one. As large and as beautiful as it was, it was always a bit intimidating to me.

On the one hand, the grandeur of that Bible drew me to it. On the other hand, the sheer mystery of it made me feel like it was too grand for me to understand in any way. Yet I could not dismiss the magnetic pull of the Scriptures. At the age of about ten years old,

I remember lying in my bed and hearing a voice deep in my spirit say to me, "Get up and read the Bible that's on your mom and dad's dresser." In our home, the Bible was respected, but we never opened it unless we were imitating and pretending to be priests, chanting the Scriptures in Greek just to make each other laugh. But this night was different. There was a literal voice pulling me toward the Scriptures.

So, I woke my mom up in the middle of the night, and I said, "Hey, Mom, if God tells you to read the Bible and you don't do it, is it a sin?" Well, the question shook her to the core. I don't know if she thought I'd lost my mind or that God was actually speaking to me. Even though we did not know the Lord intimately at the time, there was still a reverence and respect for His name and His Word. My mom's reply was typical of her passionate Greek personality. She said, "Well, get up and go read it."

So, I grabbed the Bible, went into my parents' bathroom of all places, shut the door, and began to read the Scriptures. But this time was different. This time the voice of God, the reality of God in the moment, and the Scriptures were colliding right in front of me and all around me. Today I know that voice as the one that you and I have been speaking about all this time in this book. It was the voice of the Holy Spirit.

> *When I'm walking with You, Holy Spirit, I know that I don't have to worry about missing something You want to tell me. Thank You that You will always speak to me in a way I can hear. Thank You that You don't make it hard or complicated to hear what You're saying. I open my heart and my spirit to Your voice.*

28

Our Teacher

Jesus promised us that after He departed and went back to Heaven we would not be alone. He promised to send another, and He said, speaking of the Holy Spirit, that this person would become our teacher. Jesus said He would remind us of everything that Jesus ever told us (see John 14:15–18,26).

I'm often complimented after I teach the Bible. People wonder, "How does Michael see what he sees in the Scriptures? How do these things come to light? I've never read the Scriptures that way before." Well, I have had the best teacher in the universe: the Holy Spirit. When I read the Bible, I always pray this prayer, and I do it with my children in our devotionals too. I say: *Holy Spirit, be our teacher. Please show me Jesus as I read Your Word.*

We have to remember the Scriptures tell us that all Scripture is inspired by God (see 2 Tim. 3:16). So, what better place or person to go to for a Bible study than the author of the Scriptures, the Holy Spirit? The Bible says in First Corinthians 2:12: *"Now we have received, not the spirit of the world, but the Spirit who is from God, that we might know the things that have been freely given to us by God."* The Bible is full of promises that have been freely given to us by our Heavenly Father, but entering into them requires the work of the Holy Spirit. He teaches us the Bible so that we might know Jesus.

Thank You for giving us Your written Word. I love being able to open my Bible daily and sink into the truth of Your Scriptures. I need You to be my teacher, Holy Spirit. Would You guide me to a verse You would have me meditate on today?

29

A Friend of the Holy Spirit

The Bible tells us, *"As many as are led by the Spirit of God, these are the sons of God. For you did not receive the spirit of bondage again to fear, but you received the Spirit of adoption by whom we cry out, 'Abba, Father'"* (Rom. 8:14–15).

The greatest way to become aware of the fatherly love that God has for all of us is to become a friend of the Holy Spirit. As He leads us, we receive the love of the Father.

Imagine Jesus saying, "Don't follow Me, because where I'm going, you can't go." He told them, "But the Holy Ghost, He will guide you. He will lead you" (see John 16:13). The Lord was preparing the disciples for the life that they would have to live once Jesus ascended into Heaven. Because He is so loving, He did not want them to be shocked about His departure.

Now, I can hear you asking, "Wait, I have Jesus. He's in my heart. He's everywhere." That's true, but how is He in your heart and how does He make Himself available everywhere? By His Spirit. "But the Holy Ghost, He will guide you" (see John 16:13). One of the ways the Holy Spirit teaches us is by guiding us.

> *I want to learn what it means to be Your friend, Holy Spirit. I want to recognize Your presence, learn what brings You joy, understand Your heart, and commune with You daily. You are my greatest gift. I'm so grateful for Your guidance.*

30

The Greatest Guide

My favorite pastime is fishing. Even though I played professional golf, if I had to choose between fishing and golf today, it would be fishing. My father owned boats so I grew up on the water. I was raised in a town that was on the beautiful Gulf of Mexico. Just about every day I was out on the water fishing. I even drove to other cities to fish, and slept in my car. I waded through swamps and lagoons, cut my feet on oysters, read fishing magazines—you name it and I did it to catch more fish.

One of the best things you can do as a fisherman to become familiar with uncharted waters is to be on the boat with a guide. The guide takes you to all of the good spots. His job is not to take you about the water aimlessly or drive you into a storm. The job of the guide is to show you those spots about which most people just don't know. His motives are good. He drives the boat, he knows the weather, he knows the tides, and most importantly, he knows how to find the fish.

Reading the Scriptures with the Holy Spirit is just like this. He takes you out into the water of the Scriptures, the vast ocean of truth, and then based on what you need, He begins to guide you to the different verses that become alive to you. He begins to show you Jesus in a way that you have never seen Him before. He brings you into a peaceful place, just like the guide on a boat avoids the storm. He knows the weather of your heart, just like that guide knows the weather in the area. His presence comes in waves and flows, just like that guide knows the tides. The Holy Spirit is the greatest guide on earth and in Heaven.

So, once I opened that Bible as a little boy, a relationship with the Lord began. The Holy Spirit began to answer my questions, and He would one day bring me to a place where I would hear the Gospel for the first time. But I was getting to know Him better, and to this day, that voice remains. It has become clearer and is a greater part of my life than I could ever explain.

> *You are always guiding me. I want to always be surrendered to Your leading. Help me, Holy Spirit, to quiet myself enough to hear Your prompting. Where do You want to lead me today? What do You want to talk about? What do You want to show me about Yourself?*

31

Still Waters

Maybe you are stressed; perhaps you're full of fear and anxiety? Maybe you don't sleep well anymore? Maybe your thoughts have gotten the best of you? Have you wondered if you'll ever just be the "old you" again? Wondered if you'll ever have your personality back? If you'll ever smile again, laugh with your friends, and see the good in life? Wondered if you'll ever be able to control your mind? The Bible says, *"He leads me beside still waters. He restores my soul"* (Ps. 23:2-3 ESV).

The beautiful thing about the Holy Spirit is that as He teaches and guides us, He actually heals us. He leads us to a certain place; it is the place of still waters, a place of peace, a place of tranquility. And once He leads us to these still waters, He restores our soul. Our emotions are healed. Our will is surrendered to Him. Our mind becomes the mind of Christ, all because the Holy Spirit now is driving the boat of our life. He does not desire to lead us into chaos but rather to still waters. Still waters are deep waters, and it's in those depths of peace where you will find your healing. While He is all-powerful, we must remember that He is a gentle teacher and a gentle guide who will never force His will on us or drive us. Slave masters drive; the Holy Spirit guides.

Much of the brokenness, and the pain, and the scatteredness that we go through is often due to our desire to live our lives according to the ways of the world. But the Bible teaches in First Corinthians 2:13: *"These things we also speak, not in words which man's wisdom teaches but which the Holy Spirit teaches, comparing spiritual things with spiritual."* When the Holy Spirit comes into your life, you begin to live according to another world, another kingdom. We begin to follow another voice. Our thoughts become spiritual. The eyes of the heart begin to look above. As Paul said, "I press on toward the high call of God in Christ" (see Phil. 3:14). This all comes from allowing the Holy Spirit to teach us.

Holy Spirit, I need You today. I bring to You all of the anxiety, the pain, and the disappointment that I've been carrying. I surrender these emotions to You. Lead me to the place of peace. I don't want to be the one managing my own life. I need You to teach me, to guide, and to heal me.

32

HE LEADS US INTO ALL TRUTH

Remember, Jesus said He wouldn't just guide us, but He would guide us into all truth (see John 16:13). Fear has gripped millions of lives. It has shattered families, marriages, and children. If allowed to take root, fear can literally cripple us. Fear comes from believing a lie, and it increases as we meditate on that lie. The Holy Spirit promises to lead us into all truth—not merely to speak truth to us, but to lead us into truth.

Yes, He's a faithful guide. There are so many examples of this in the Bible. Do you remember Peter on the rooftop of Simon the Tanner? The Scripture says, "*...the Spirit said to him, 'Behold, three men are seeking you. Arise therefore, go down and go with them, doubting nothing; for I have sent them'*" (Acts 10:19–20). Peter recognized the voice of the Holy Spirit and yielded to Him. Again we see this happening in the life of Paul through the Macedonian call. The Holy Spirit spoke to Paul in a dream. A man stood there begging him to come bring the Gospel. Paul obeyed, went to Macedonia, and preached the glorious Gospel.

How about Philip and the Ethiopian eunuch? There Philip goes to Gaza. He sees an Ethiopian reading the Book of Isaiah. He runs to the chariot to tell that man about the Gospel. Why did he run? The Holy Spirit urged him to run. Philip was getting caught up in the Holy Spirit's desire to get the Gospel to that man. And after that man believed on Jesus, Philip baptized him, and that man took the Gospel to Ethiopia. Today, Ethiopia is a Christian nation. I've seen hundreds of thousands of Orthodox and Coptic Christians and Evangelicals burning to know God all because Philip listened to the Guide—the wonderful Guide—the Holy Spirit.

Sometimes my fears loom so large in front of me, Holy Spirit. You have promised to lead me into all truth, Holy Spirit, and my confidence is in You. I will quiet my heart so I can hear You, and I will trust You to guide me where I am supposed to go today.

33

By the Spirit

Perhaps you've said to yourself, "What do I have to offer? What can I bring the world? I'm just an average person. I don't have a great education. I barely know the Bible. I have no theological training. I'm incredibly normal." You are the exact type of person the Holy Spirit enjoys using.

Once we are convinced of our inability, it is then that He steps in to give us power. The Scripture says it is *"not by might nor by power, but by My Spirit,' says the Lord"* (Zech. 4:6). The Lord takes average people and quickens them, just like He empowered Philip, Peter, and Paul to shake regions of the earth. Through the life of Paul, Asia Minor and Europe were Christianized. Between these three men, many nations of the world followed and continued to follow Jesus because of one reason: They yielded to the guiding presence of the Holy Spirit and obeyed His word. And you can do the same.

How do you begin? Begin talking to Him. Begin asking questions. Begin waiting upon and listening to Him. Give Him time to talk back to you. Become familiar with His slightest nudge, His slightest whisper, and His faithful presence. He will take your life and change the world with it.

I'm so aware of my weaknesses and limitations, Holy Spirit. But I know that You are the one that qualifies those You call. So, I offer myself up to Your plans for the world. I am yielded to Your presence. Where are You moving in my life today? How can I become more aware of You in this moment?

34

The Spirit of Prayer

When you talk about the Holy Spirit with people and all of the amazing things that He does every single day, you rarely hear people mention the Holy Spirit and His role in prayer. If you do and you are from Charismatic-Pentecostal circles, you may hear a little bit about the gift of tongues, but there is so much more that the beautiful person of the Holy Spirit does in us as it pertains to prayer.

In order for us to understand His role in prayer, we have to determine what prayer is and what prayer is not. I grew up hearing that prayer is a humble request made known to God. I don't completely disagree with that, but it is only a partial truth. What is the core of prayer? What is prayer itself? Let's have a look at what the Bible has to say about prayer and the Holy Spirit. Remember, He is the Spirit of prayer.

Zechariah 12:10 says He is the *"Spirit of grace and prayer,"* or *"grace and supplication"* (Zech. 12:10 NLT, NIV). Another way to read that is He is the Spirit who empowers prayer, or He is the Spirit of empowering prayer. In Psalm 109:4, God gives us an amazing picture of what is available in the Holy Spirit. Listen to the words of David: "Though I love them, they stand accusing me like satan for what I've never done. I will pray until I become prayer itself" (see Ps. 109:4).

Can you sense the Lord changing your view of prayer? I believe you will discover the beautiful truth of our absolute dependence on and need for the Holy Spirit and a life of prayer. Prayer is not only something; at the core it is Someone.

Bishop Kallistos Ware of the Greek Orthodox Church says, "'When you pray,' it has been wisely said by an Orthodox writer in Finland, 'you yourself must be silent.... You yourself must be silent; let the prayer speak.'" He goes on to say, "The one who learns to be still in the presence of the Lord and listens begins to listen to the voice of prayer in his own heart; and he understands that this voice is not his own but that of another speaking within him."

Help me to quiet my mind, Holy Spirit. I want to still any racing thoughts, any anxiety creeping into my mind. I release any semblance of control that I am holding onto, consciously or subconsciously. I want to commune with You. I want to hear Your voice so clearly.

35

Our Source of Life

In Luke 11:1, the disciples come to the Lord after they see the Lord praying, and they say, *"Lord, teach us to pray, just as John taught his disciples"* (NIV). This is a loaded passage. First of all, the disciples were inspired to pray because they saw Jesus praying. If you want to inspire others to pray, more than you telling them to pray, they really need to see you praying. A life of prayer in our own lives will inspire a life of prayer in the lives of others.

Looking back on my life, those who have impacted me the most are those who have lived a life of prayer. Their experience of God was visible to me as I interacted with them, and it was clear that whatever was happening in their prayer room was changing their lives and making Jesus more real to them than anything else. This is exactly what happened with the disciples. They saw Jesus praying and saw the life He lived, and they understood that whatever was happening when He was alone with the Father was the source of His life. And so, they came to Him after He prayed, wanting to learn how to pray.

Notice they said, *"Lord, teach us to pray"* (Luke 11:1). They did not say, "Lord, teach us to heal. Teach us to cast out devils. Show us how to do that walking-on-the-water thing."

They knew that it was not about how-to methods but about the Holy Spirit resting on Jesus and remaining. And after Jesus told them in John 5 that He did nothing that He did not see the Father do (see John 5:19), they began to understand that there was a deep, unbreakable eternal connection between Him and His Father. They wanted the same. They knew that was the epicenter of all they saw with their eyes.

Holy Spirit, teach me to love You and focus on Your Presence. Teach me to listen to Your voice. I want to obey You.

36

Praying vs. Saying

Prayer is not so much something we do; rather, it is the activity and the person of the Spirit of prayer. What is more important in the area of discipleship than teaching people to connect with God?

Jesus' response when the disciples asked Him to teach them to pray is beautiful and very telling. Notice there is no hesitation. Also, it's important to see that Jesus answers directly. That tells me that this is a question He wanted to answer. It was a question that He was waiting on them to ask because it was important to Him. There were other moments when He answered back, when He answered their questions with a question. It seemed like He often would speak in riddles and parables when the disciples came with a genuine question. Not this time. This time He was clear and direct. I believe this was something He longed for them to understand.

Jesus answered by saying, "*When you pray, say…*" (Luke 11:2). Notice there's a comma between "pray" and "say." If you're going to spend any extended time alone with the Lord, you will discover that there is a huge difference between *praying* and *saying*, and this Scripture shows that beautifully. It is very important that before we begin to say and request things in prayer, we allow prayer to begin. Once prayer begins, we can begin to "say" in faith.

Benny Hinn once said, "If I have ten minutes to pray, I worship for nine." This is a beautiful truth. Allow the activity of the Spirit to moisten the moment with the dew of faith so that the seeds we sow in our words can take root in fertile soil. I have learned this to be true as I pray for the sick. I like to wait a moment and allow the presence of God to become more real to me than the sickness. I have found that oftentimes faith is available in a very special way in such a time. Why is this? Because faith is not something; it is Someone. The Bible calls the Holy Spirit the Spirit of faith (see 2 Cor. 4:13). Well, the same is true with prayer. Prayer is not something; rather, it is Someone. It's the Holy Spirit.

Holy Spirit, I want to know You deeply. Teach me Your ways. Your Presence is Life.

37

A LIVING LETTER

Bishop Kallistos Ware says, "In prayer it is the divine partner, and not the human, who takes the initiative and it is the divine partner, the Holy Spirit, whose action is fundamental." Saint Gregory of Sinai said regarding prayer, "Prayer is God, who works all things in all men." Notice his statement here: "Prayer is God working." Now, I wouldn't go so far as to say that, but I understand what he's saying. True prayer, if it is truly the Holy Spirit, is to be joined and not worked up. It is not something that I initiate but something that I join. It's not something I do; it is something that I am swept into like a river.

The Bible says that we are invited to *"drink from the river of* [the Lord's] *delights"* (Ps. 36:8 ESV). Once you begin to understand that prayer is the activity of the Spirit and not the activity of man, it can be joined with joy and ease. Listen to Paul's words: "It is not I but Christ in me" (see Gal. 2:20). He understood that the experience of God did not depend on him but rather on the internal presence of the Holy Spirit within him.

The words of John the Baptist do apply to the life of prayer: *"He must increase, but I must decrease"* (John 3:30). That is why I can be silent and still pray. In fact, I can be praying while I'm preaching. The greatest meetings I've ever had have been those meetings where two conversations are going on: one, with me and the Holy Spirit, and two, with me and the people. The experience that people have in the seats often depends on the experience I am having with the Lord. My goal is to let my words be His words and His words be my words. What I am really experiencing then is prayer.

You don't ever have to stop praying. Paul said, *"Praying always... in the Spirit"* (Eph. 6:18 KJV). Is he speaking about the gift of tongues? Partially; there is much more to praying in the Spirit than speaking in tongues. Praying in the Spirit is to be overcome by, to be filled with, and to join the activity in the Spirit until your life becomes a prayer. Again, Paul said that we are living epistles (see 2 Cor. 3:2). What does he mean by that? He means that somebody who has been given over to God and possessed by the Holy Spirit literally becomes a living letter before men and before Heaven. In other words, if people don't know what God is like and do not know the will of God, your life becomes a living letter that paints a beautiful picture of God before them and literally teaches them the will of God. You become a pen and a letter in the hands of the Holy Spirit Himself.

I'm so grateful that You haven't made it hard to pray. You invite me to drink from the river of Your presence, to experience Your delight, and to commune with You throughout every moment of my day. I turn from any limited way I've thought of prayer, Holy Spirit. I want to join with You seamlessly until my life becomes a prayer.

38

A Manifestation of Our Salvation

Kallistos Ware also said, "Prayer is to stop talking and to listen to the wordless voice of God within our heart; it is to cease doing things on our own, and to enter into the action of God." I absolutely love that statement. There are many ways to pray, but I am dealing with the core of prayer here, the foundation—that prayer itself is the presence and activity of God in us until we are completely taken over by the activity of the Holy Spirit.

I hope you're discovering that prayer is impossible without the Holy Spirit. More importantly, I hope you're discovering that with the Holy Spirit, you enter the very action of God. What a privilege, what a joy, and what an opportunity.

The whole point of the Christian life is to love Jesus. It is to live on and off of the same presence that saved us. The same experience that brought us into the Kingdom is meant to be the food that keeps us alive while in the Kingdom. In other words, it was the experience of God, the coming of the Holy Spirit showing us Jesus, when we were born again that brought us salvation. Now we are to live in and from the same presence as we experience salvation.

When we enter true prayer, it is a manifestation of our salvation, our union with God. After all, that's why Jesus died. We desperately need the Holy Spirit to teach us to pray. We need His direction. We need His voice. We need His expertise. Job 37:19 says, *"Teach us what we shall say to Him; we cannot arrange our case because of darkness"* (NASB). In other words, I have nothing to say to God right now. I need the Holy Spirit.

> *You have invited me into union with You, Lord, and You've given me Your Spirit to teach me how to fully live in and from Your presence. Will You teach me what to say today? I want to stop doing things—including prayer—on my own. What is on Your heart today, Holy Spirit? How can I become a vessel for Your delight?*

39

A United Cry

Romans 8:26 says, "*In the same way the Spirit also helps our weakness; for we do not know how to pray as we should, but the Spirit Himself intercedes for us with groanings too deep for words*" (NASB). This verse teaches us many amazing things regarding the Spirit of prayer. Number one: "*The Spirit…helps our weakness*" (Rom. 8:26 NASB). Many of us are often weak—physically, mentally, and spiritually. The Holy Spirit promises to come and help us in our weakness and make us strong.

The Scripture says, "*Let the weak say, 'I am strong'*" (Joel 3:10). Number two: When we don't know how to pray, "*the Spirit Himself intercedes for us with groanings too deep for words*" (Rom. 8:26 NASB). When we don't know how to pray, He prays for us. Again, this is much deeper than praying in tongues. This is a depth of prayer that is too deep for words. It is when our flesh cries out, as David said, *"for the living God"* (Ps. 84:2).

The Holy Spirit tells us that we belong to our Father. Galatians 4:6 says, *"And because you are sons, God has sent forth the Spirit of His Son into your hearts, crying out, 'Abba, Father!'"* Just think, the Holy Spirit Himself cries out for the Father as He lives in you. Romans 8:15 says, *"Ye have not received the spirit of bondage again to fear; but ye have received the Spirit of adoption, whereby we cry, Abba, Father"* (KJV). This is a beautiful truth: these two cries become one—our cry becomes His cry, and His cry becomes our cry. This is a manifestation of Paul's words: *"He who is joined to the Lord is one spirit with Him"* (1 Cor. 6:17). Prayer is the experience of the activity of the Holy Spirit, and the result is this merging of cries, whereby we experience being one with the Lord.

I want to commune with You, Holy Spirit, but so often I feel like I'm missing the mark. I am weak, but You have promised to be strong. I rest in Your promise. Mingle the cry of my heart with Yours.

40

Give Yourself to Prayer

Maybe you say, "I'm too tired to pray." Not anymore. Now that you've read this, you've found that the Spirit is the answer. He is prayer itself. Remember the words of Jesus when the disciples were sleeping in the Garden of Gethsemane? He said to them, *"The spirit indeed is willing, but the flesh is weak"* (Matt. 26:41; Mark 14:38). Maybe the reason you've become so tired is that you've been doing too much in prayer. You've been activating your flesh. You've been pacing, walking, shouting. That can be of God at times, but many times it's not.

Sometimes the Lord just wants us to sit there, find what He's doing in the moment, and yield our body and our will to His plan. The Spirit is always willing. So, what is the key? Join the Spirit. Madame Guyon said, "Prayer has now become easy, sweet, and delightful." All who desire to pray may pray without difficulty because we can be strengthened by the grace of the Holy Spirit. Again, Madam Guyon said, "God, is only to be found in our inner selves, which is the holy of holies where God dwells."

My prayer for you is that you will enjoy and yield to the master of prayer Himself, to prayer itself, the Holy Spirit. Instead of bringing a list of our plans to God, why don't we just have a seat in the morning with a cup of coffee and our Bibles, and pray the prayer below? Prayer will become a continual, divine, face-to-face love dance with Jesus Himself.

Holy Spirit, You're the Spirit of prayer. Where do You want to go this morning? What do You want to do? I know You want to show me Jesus because You love Him more than I do. So, I'm here, Lord, to see Him. How do You want me to see Him? What side of Him do You want me to see? I trust You, Lord, with my problems. I trust You with my concerns. But right now, I come to You for You and You alone.

41

An Invitation to Trial

I used to believe that if I lived a life of prayer, fasting, devotion, and obedience to the Lord, I would not suffer and go through difficult trials in my life. I am sure God was probably laughing at my mind-set. Now I know that such a life is basically an invitation to testing and trials. In fact, the opposite is true: living a life after Jesus is a guarantee that we will go through difficulty.

The Lord told us that we are no greater than our Master and that if they hated Him, they will hate us (see John 15:20). I love Peter's perspective in First Peter chapter 1, verse 7. He says, "*The trial of your faith, being much more precious than of gold that perisheth, though it be tried with fire, might be found unto praise and honour and glory at the appearing of Jesus Christ"* (1 Pet. 1:7 KJV). Again, he says, in First Peter chapter 5, verse 10, *"But the God of all grace, who hath called us unto his eternal glory by Christ Jesus, after that ye have suffered a while, make you perfect, stablish, strengthen, settle you"* (KJV).

I am not telling you that all suffering comes from God. I think part of the confusion is what we mean when we say "suffering." Let me very clear: Everything that comes our way in life is not from God. Sickness is not from God. Depression is not from God. Lack is not from God. Rejection, shame, anger, hatred, are not from God. However, Jesus said that we would be persecuted for righteousness' sake. He also said that many people in our lives would reject us and come against us because of our walk with Him (see John 15:18). The Bible is very clear that if we walk with Jesus, we will go through trials. After all, nobody lived a more beautiful, loving, and peaceful life than Jesus did. And yet, He suffered more pain than anyone.

> *Precious Lord, trials are a promise from You. You said they would come. Make me more like Jesus in the midst of difficulty. Soften my heart when I am persecuted. Thank You for the privilege of the cross.*

42

His Presence Is Food

I have seen time and time again those who once loved the Lord, lived peaceful lives, wanted unity and so much more, slowly but surely live lives outside the presence of God. They begin to spend more time on themselves and the supposedly important work they are doing than alone in the secret place with the Lord. This begins to resurrect old ways, old perspectives, and the old hardness of heart, which gives way to motives that are not pure, and little by little these motives and ways supersede the ways of the Holy Spirit. For example, when you're walking in the presence of God, you're not interested in promoting yourself because you are constantly feasting on the Lord. You have no need to be recognized by people because your main objective is to experience the Holy Spirit. His presence becomes your literal food.

Think of this for a moment: In John chapter 4, Jesus goes to Samaria and sits by a well and meets a woman there. He ministers to her privately. All the while, the disciples cannot find Him. So, there Jesus is, ministering to the woman at the well, one on one, and the disciples cannot find Him. Perhaps they thought He'd be with the crowds, but He wasn't. He was alone with a person who needed help. When they found Him, they ran up to Him and said, "*Rabbi, eat*" (John 4:31). He said to them, "*I have food to each of which you do not know*" (John 4:32). What did Jesus mean by this? What was He saying? He explains it in verse 34: the Lord said, "*My food is to do the will of Him who sent Me to accomplish His work*" (John 4:34 NASB).

Jesus lived before the Father, whether He was on the shores of Galilee with tens of thousands in front of Him for a great miracle service, sitting by the well with one woman, or on the mountain completely by Himself praying. He did not live before man. He lived before God. Because of that, He ate the food of the will of God, which is the presence of God. Therefore, He was completely fulfilled. He never had to manipulate, promote, or wiggle Himself into some situation so that people would know Him better. He simply enjoyed the presence of the Father and obeyed the voice of the Father. The result of this was a life that shook the world in three years.

Keep me close to You, Holy Spirit. I want to walk so in sync with You that when I step away from You with my attention, I can feel the departure acutely. I want Your guidance. Nothing is more important to me than walking with Your presence.

43

OUR COMFORTER

I have had to make some tough choices in my life that have led to ridicule and isolation. Time and time again, I have chosen the presence of God over money and notoriety. I have chosen the smile of Jesus over the applause of man. This has often caused conflict and persecution. My heart has been so broken that there have been mornings when I have wondered if I could get through the day. I have felt the pain of rejection. I know what it is to be maligned behind my back to leaders I respect, all because I refuse to compromise. This is the type of suffering and persecution that Jesus promised us.

To be real, this is very minor in comparison to what millions of Christians face around the world. They know true suffering. They know true pain. As real as ours is, it's important that we remember that much of the Christian population is not even allowed to gather in public due to fear of being killed or losing family members. Our brothers and sisters in the Middle East are a perfect example of this.

I remember a story that touched my heart. My father-in-law was telling Rex Humbard about all the persecution he was going through. Rex, being the gentle, loving father that he was, just sat there and listened. When my father-in-law was done, Rex looked at him and said, "Benny, look down at your hands." And so, he did. Rex went on to say, "Do you see any holes in them?" and gently smiled.

What was the point? As painful as our persecution can be, as painful as our suffering can be, take comfort in the fact that One suffered a much greater trial and endured much more brutal pain than we ever did, and His name is Jesus. It's in these moments, however, that we need a Comforter. We all need to feel the peace of God and the embrace of God in moments when people or situations bring trial, confusion, and pain.

Thank You, Holy Spirit, that You bring both comfort to my soul. Whenever I am in pain, I can turn to You and experience Your peace, Your tender love, and Your protection. But I am also reminded that I am not alone. Jesus, You suffered in every way that I have. I look to You for fellowship as I face difficult challenges.

44

He Brings to Remembrance

I like to compare feeling the peace of God to being hurt physically and showing up to a good hospital. Picture the wound in your body as the wound in your heart or your mind. The nurses are like the angels. They're rushing around to protect you, to make sure your vitals are functioning properly, to make sure that nobody's in the room who's not supposed to be there. And then eventually in walks this doctor in a white jacket with a smile on his face. He comes and puts his hand on your shoulder. Before he says anything, his reassuring smile brings peace to your soul. The hospital is much like the Kingdom of God. The suffering and hurting people of the world run in, and they are tended to, to be healed and to get up again. Jesus is the One who, no matter what we face, is always there to bring us peace.

Second Corinthians chapter 1, verses 3 and 4, say, *"Blessed be the God and Father of our Lord Jesus Christ, the Father of mercies and God of all comfort, who comforts us in all our affliction so that we will be able to comfort those who are in any affliction with the comfort with which we ourselves are comforted by God"* (NASB). God is a God of comfort. In fact, one of the names for the Holy Spirit is Comforter. John 14:26 says, *"But the Comforter, which is the Holy Ghost, whom the Father will send in My name, he shall teach you all things, and bring all things to your remembrance, whatsoever I have said unto you"* (KJV). Now maybe you're saying, "I need comfort, not remembrance. I need peace, not a reminder." Remember, the words of Jesus carry life in them.

Sometimes our suffering is due to a lack of vision and proper perspective. How we see things frames our world. The Bible says, *"As* [a man] *thinketh in his heart, so he is"* (Prov. 23:7 KJV). There are many times when I have suffered greatly and the slightest adjustment in my perspective literally eliminated the pain in my heart. The moment I saw things from God's perspective, or even instead of mine, things changed. One of the ways the Holy Spirit comforts us is by bringing to remembrance what Jesus said.

It's so easy for me to forget Your goodness, Your faithfulness, and the promises You've made over my life. I slip so easily into thinking I need to make everything happen on my own, but that only leads to anxiety and isolation. I need to be reminded, Holy Spirit. Help me to remember Your faithfulness and Presence.

45

His Presence Comforts

Another way the Holy Spirit brings comfort is by His presence alone. I can't tell you how many times I have been stressed and afraid, and I'll hear this small voice in my heart say, "Stop what you're doing and worship Me. Just give Me a moment to touch you." I personally believe that the experience of Holy Spirit is just a whisper away, and His presence comes and settles our chaos. He wraps Himself around us like this blanket of peace, and without hearing any audible voice, there's a deep knowledge that everything is going to be okay. Acts 9:31 says, *"So the church throughout all Judea and Galilee and Samaria enjoyed peace, being built up; and going on in the fear of the Lord and in the comfort of the Holy Spirit..."* (NASB). There's something about the comfort of the Holy Spirit that changes everything.

Have you ever been so busy and scattered in your mind that things just seem to get out of control? Are there people in your life whom you can't seem to corral? Are there areas of life that have gotten away from you and that are moving at such a fast speed that you can't get your arms around them? You're trying and trying to keep up with the demands of life, but the faster you run, the more the demands outpace you. You throw your hands up in the air and say, "I don't know what to do anymore. I can't do this." And instead of you reigning in life as the Bible says (see Rom. 5:17), life begins to reign over you. Yet amid all of that noise and movement, deep within you there seems to be this voice, and the voice says, "Stop what you're doing, and just give Me a second. Stop what you're doing, and say My name. Stop what you're doing, and worship Me." That's the voice of the Holy Spirit.

He's not trying to get you to stop what you're doing for the mere purpose of stopping, but He understands that in that pause, a doorway is created for Him to step into your situation to comfort you. He wants you to be okay. And as you stop, He moves. Where does He move? Toward you. And the minute He comes your way and puts His hand on you like that doctor puts his hand on that sick patient, He brings you peace. Once He brings you peace, He begins to move into that situation and we oftentimes forget to give Him the green light. His green light comes from our red light. The moment we stop for Him, He moves for us.

I am going to take this moment to stop my strategizing, to put a pause on all of my planning, and to release my attempt to get control over my situation. I am giving myself to You. Holy Spirit, would You come and comfort me? Would You show me how You see me? Please let me know Your peaceful touch.

46

He Is a Person

Like the Father and the Son, the Holy Spirit has many names and characteristics. After all, He is a person. If there were one truth that I pray you would be possessed with, it would be this: The Holy Spirit is a person who can be known. If He is a person, that means He has a personality. He enjoys some things, and others He does not. There are certain people that He is closer to than others. It might make us a bit uncomfortable, but the reality is that God has favorites. If it were not so, He would not have favor. His favorites are covered with favor. Of course He feels closer to some people than others. It's because He can trust them—and not just trust them with what He does; He can trust them with His feelings.

One of the ways He begins a relationship is by sharing His character with us. It's sort of like an introduction. He begins to show us what He's like and who He is. It's no different than you meeting somebody and saying, "Hello" and giving that person your name. Once you've sat down and taken some time with that person, you would begin to talk to them about who you are, your history, what you like, and what you don't like. He or she would then discover your character and your personality if you continue the relationship.

This is no different than meeting the Holy Spirit, except He's more wonderful than anybody else you've ever met in your life. In Isaiah 11:2, He begins to share with us seven beautiful characteristics of His person. We call this the "sevenfold Spirit of God." Now, there are many other angles by which we see the Holy Spirit. He has many more names, but these seven are a beautiful place to begin exploring the depths of the Holy Spirit's character.

Isaiah 11:2 says, *"And the spirit of the Lord shall rest on him, the spirit of wisdom and understanding, the spirit of counsel and might, the spirit of knowledge and of the fear of the Lord"* (KJV). The sevenfold Spirit here is: 1) the Spirit of the Lord, 2) the Spirit of wisdom, 3) the Spirit of understanding, 4) the Spirit of counsel, 5) the Spirit of might, 6) the Spirit of knowledge, and 7) the Spirit of the fear of the Lord.

> *Thank You, Holy Spirit, for making Yourself accessible to me. I want to know all about You. I want to know what delights Your heart and what grieves You. I want to become a student of Your character. As I dwell on these attributes, will You reveal Yourself to me in greater measure?*

47

The Spirit of the Lord

It is vital that we understand that the Holy Spirit is the Spirit of the Lord. He is not beneath the Father or the Son. While He is His own person, He is still completely one with Them. Three in One—this is the mystery and beauty of the Trinity. The Holy Spirit is the Spirit of Jesus, and the Holy Spirit is the Spirit of the Father. The Holy Spirit is the Spirit of the Lord. The Bible says, *"Now the Lord is that Spirit..."* (2 Cor. 3:17 KJV).

While He is our friend, we have to remember that He is our Lord. He must be in charge of our lives. He is to lead the dance. Of course, He is the most loving person on planet Earth today. Yes, He is the most intimate being you will ever meet. He loves it when we cooperate with Him. He wants us to co-labor with Him. He loves to have conversations with us. He's a beautiful friend; there is no doubt about it. However, we need to remember that He is God Almighty, the Creator of Heaven and earth.

Even the apostles knew this, as evidenced by the Nicene Creed. The Creed has become a foundational statement for the Church worldwide. Listen to what the apostles said regarding the Holy Spirit in the early Church: "We believe in the Holy Spirit, the Lord, the Giver of life, who proceeds from the Father, who with the Father and the Son is worshiped and glorified, who has spoken through the prophets."

Since the Church began, the Holy Spirit has been known as the Spirit of the Lord. The Greek word for *Lord* is the word *kyrios*. It means "one who completely owns something." So, to say that the Holy Spirit is Lord of my life is to say that He completely owns every ounce of my being. It means that He has the right to tell me what to do and what not to do. He can tell me not to go somewhere. He can tell me whom to marry. He's allowed to say "no" to me. In other words, my life is not my own if the Holy Spirit is to be my Lord.

I believe in You, Holy Spirit, the Lord, the Giver of life, who proceeds from the Father and the Son, who with the Father and the Son is worshiped and glorified, who has spoken through the prophets. You are my dearest friend, closer than my own breath. You are the Lord over my life. I am surrendered completely to You.

48

OBEDIENCE

One day I was sitting with Reinhard Bonnke over lunch, and he began to tell me the story of how the Lord blessed his ministry with a rent-free office building in Orlando. It housed the headquarters of Christ for all Nations and saved them tens of thousands of dollars per month. The story I'm about to share with you has been shared by Reinhard around the world. One day the Lord spoke to Reinhard and said, "Reinhard, I am going to give you a harvest home." He said, "Lord, what does that mean—a harvest home?" Instantly, the Lord put on his heart, "I will give you a building, a headquarters, so that you can house the needs of the ministry, the staff, and raise up evangelists to go around the world."

Immediately, Reinhard got on the phone and called his staff. "I want you to get ready. I am driving in to go look at buildings. Find me a realtor." Being a Saturday morning, it was very difficult to find a realtor, not to mention that the Christ for all Nations staff was off for the weekend. They drove around and did not find a building. Many people would think that it was a failed day, that Reinhard might have been better off just enjoying his Saturday doing something a little more relaxing, but he had a different perspective.

He said, "I drove in on a minute's notice knowing I wouldn't find a place today, but I wanted God to see that when the Holy Spirit speaks to me, I obey, and that I jump at His voice." Hearing that story changed my life. Reinhard looked me in the eye, and he said, "God does not just wait for us to obey, but He watches to see how quickly we obey. And I want God to know that when He speaks to me, I jump with obedience." This is somebody who knows the Holy Spirit is not only his friend, but the Lord Himself.

I'm so grateful for examples of leaders who have exemplified radical obedience in their lives. I want to live like that. Today, I lay down anything—my reputation, my dignity, my control, my assumptions—that would stand in the way of me jumping to obedience when You speak. Holy Spirit, what would You have me do today?

49

Childlike Trust

Following the Holy Spirit is about having a childlike trust in Him as a good Lord. The most simple act of obedience can change somebody's life forever. Jesus is like that, you know? Remember when He multiplied the fish and the bread. Before He did, He said, "Put them in groups of fifty and one hundred" (see Mark 6:39). Why? I don't know. Just because He wanted to. There are so many beautiful examples of the Lord asking us to do things that seem absolutely insignificant, and yet He uses them to be bridges that connect Heaven and earth in a second.

There is a passage in the Book of Acts that I absolutely love because I have found the principle it reveals to be true in daily life, in the ministry, and in a friendship with the Holy Spirit. The Bible shares an amazing truth with us in Acts 8:

> *Now an angel of the Lord said to Philip, "Go south to the road—the desert road—that goes down from Jerusalem to Gaza." So he started out, and on his way he met an Ethiopian eunuch, an important official in charge of all the treasury of the* [queen]. *This man had gone to Jerusalem to worship, and on his way home was sitting in his chariot reading the Book of Isaiah the prophet. The Spirit told Philip, "Go to that chariot and stay near it."*
>
> *Then Philip ran up to the chariot and heard the man reading Isaiah the prophet. "Do you understand what you are reading?"* (Acts 8:26-30 NIV)

Think of this for a moment: Why would the Bible go out of the way to highlight the fact that Philip ran to chariot in verse 30? Why didn't he walk? Why didn't he sprint? Why does it specifically say he ran? It is because a person who walks with the Holy Spirit understands the importance of instant obedience to the voice of God. Had Philip walked, he would've missed the chariot, which would've meant the eunuch would not have come to the Lord and would not have taken the Gospel back to Ethiopia. Ethiopia has been a Christian nation since the first century because Phillip decided to run when he heard the Holy Spirit speak to him. He knew that the Spirit was the Lord Himself. How powerful is the combination of the voice of the Spirit of the Lord and our obedience!

I've heard many people say, "I just don't hear His voice anymore. What should I do?" I'll often ask them, "What did He say to you the last time you heard Him?" And they'll tell me. I'll reply, "Did you do what He said?" They'll say, "No." My reply is, "Why would He continue to speak and trust you with more of

His voice if you did not do what He said to do last time?" This walk with Him is not complicated. It is simple and childlike, yet full of depth and joy.

> *Forgive me, Holy Spirit, for any time You've spoken and I didn't immediately respond. I never want my own fears or doubt to get in the way of stewarding our connection and obeying Your voice. I trust You completely. I want to follow any direction You give me. Help me to return to that childlike simplicity.*

50

Trusting His No

You can trust the Holy Spirit even when He challenges you. The renewed mind begins to see a challenge as a bridge to greater breakthrough. The unrenewed mind sees a challenge from the Lord as a moment to fail. Our job is merely to obey. Once we obey the voice of the Holy Spirit, who is the Lord, He begins to take the matter into His own hands. I have seen this time and time again with healing miracles. My friend Paul Teske says, "Throw the pitch and watch God hit it." So simple but so profound.

He goes on to say, "We often think, 'Well, what if I throw a bad pitch?'" His reply is, "You can throw any pitch you want to God. If He says, 'Throw it,' throw your best pitch, and God can hit a home run. If you throw it in the dirt, He can still hit a home run. You can throw it in the backstop, and He can still hit a home run with it. But if you don't throw the pitch, you will see significantly fewer home runs from God."

I pray you begin to trust the Lord. Trust His "yes" and trust His "no." How often do we not feel peace in our hearts when we're making a decision, and sometimes we see that as God's disapproval. Many times His "no" is an approval of our life. It shows His care and His compassion for us that He doesn't want us to make mistakes. A beautiful example of this is the Macedonian call that came to Paul the apostle. Just before Paul received a calling to go to Macedonia, he received a warning from the Holy Spirit not to go to Asia.

> *They passed through the Phrygian and Galatian region, having been forbidden by the Holy Spirit to speak the word in Asia; and after they came to Mysia, they were trying to go into Bithynia, and the Spirit of Jesus did not permit them; and passing by Mysia, they came to Troas. A vision appeared to Paul in the night: a man of Macedonia was standing and appealing to him, and saying, "Come over to Macedonia and help us." When he had seen the vision, immediately we sought to go into Macedonia, concluding that God had called us to preach the gospel to them* (Acts 16:6–10 NASB).

This is a beautiful picture of the Holy Spirit functioning as our Lord. If He tells you not to do something, it is because He has something better for you to do with Him. Remember, in His will is a greater manifestation of His presence. His presence invites us into obedience, and obedience increases the measure of presence that we experience. So, in the will of God, as we listen carefully to the Holy Spirit and trust Him as our Lord, we are promised more presence, and more presence brings more satisfaction and more breakthrough.

Thank You, Holy Spirit, that You care enough about my life to tell me "no" when I need to hear it. You are not distant. You care about the intimate details of my life. I can turn to You for guidance with even the smallest decision, and I can trust Your answer is the best for me.

51

THE SPIRIT OF WISDOM

The Holy Spirit is also called the Spirit of wisdom. Acts 6:8–10 says,

> *And Stephen, full of grace and power, was performing great wonders and signs among the people. But some men from what was called the Synagogue of the Freedmen, including both Cyrenians and Alexandrians, and some from Cilicia and Asia, rose up and argued with Stephen. But they were unable to cope with the wisdom and the Spirit with which he was speaking* (NASB).

As you begin to walk in the Spirit and treasure His presence, wisdom will become yours. There's something I want you to understand: Wisdom is not something; it is Someone. It is the person of the Lord. In fact, the Bible says that "Jesus Christ is the wisdom of God" (see 1 Cor. 1:24).

Proverbs 2:2 says, "*...incline thine ear unto wisdom, and apply thine heart to understanding*" (KJV). This is simply telling us to give our ear to the voice and person of the Holy Spirit. Perhaps you're saying, "Wisdom is something, Michael. I don't agree with you. It can't be Someone." Proverbs 8:1 says, *"Does not wisdom call, and understanding lift up her voice?"* (NASB). Does a something call us? Of course not. Only a person calls.

Proverbs 8:11 says, *"For wisdom is better than jewels; and all desirable things cannot compare with her"* (NASB). Moreover, listen to what the Scripture says in Proverbs 8:12–13: *"I, wisdom, dwell with prudence and I find knowledge and discretion. The fear of the Lord is to hate evil; pride and arrogance and the evil way and the perverted mouth, I hate"* (NASB). See, wisdom here is speaking as a person.

Again, the Bible says in Proverbs 8:14–21:

> *Counsel is mine and sound wisdom; I am understanding, power is mine. By me kings reign, and rulers decree justice. By me princes rule, and nobles, all who judge rightly. I love those who love me; and those who diligently seek me will find me. Riches and honor are with me, enduring wealth and righteousness. My fruit is better than gold, even pure gold, and my yield better than the choicest silver. I walk in the way of righteousness in the midst of the paths of justice, to endow those who love me with wealth, that I may fill their treasuries* (NASB).

By the language of the Scriptures here, does this sound like some inanimate object to you or some ethereal concept? No, Wisdom is certainly a person.

Wisdom is the person of the Lord. You are the Spirit of wisdom, Holy Spirit, and You have given me access to learning about and receiving from You. All I need is to turn to You, and You will respond.

52

The Spirit of Understanding

The Spirit of understanding is an awesome aspect of the Holy Spirit. While wisdom allows us into and unites us with the very thoughts and movement of the Spirit, the Spirit of understanding opens up His ways to us. The Holy Spirit begins to open the Word of God to us, and mysteries become available in a moment. Jesus expects us to understand and comprehend His words. This will only come as a result of the Spirit of understanding moving in our lives.

Jesus said, "*For the heart of this people has become dull, with their ears they scarcely hear, and they have closed their eyes, otherwise they would see with their eyes, hear with their ears, and understand with their heart and return, and I would heal them*" (Matt. 13:15 NASB). Notice the issue here is a heart issue, not merely a mind issue. The heart is absolutely connected with our thinking. Thus, it is connected to our ability to understand.

The dull heart blinds us, deafens us, pushes us away from His presence, and keeps us emotionally sick. It is the desire of God to sensitize the heart first, then to trigger the rest of our spiritual senses. This is a spiritual issue that the Holy Spirit and He alone can fix. Once He touches the heart, He begins to open up the words of Jesus and we begin to understand the Word. Statements are no longer mere statements in the Scriptures. They lead us into an encounter with God. As we begin to understand His ways, it becomes much easier to cooperate with Him, which leads to deeper fellowship. Without the Spirit of understanding, He can speak to us and we can leave having forgotten everything He said. The culture of Heaven becomes a reality to us as we discover the treasures of His Word. Authority is birthed in certain arenas because we see His ways clearly.

Remember, a person is meant to be known, while a person's ways can be understood. It's like this: Wisdom sees the entire picture, the end from the beginning. Understanding helps us with the journey. Great visionaries often see Z from A due to wisdom flowing. They still need understanding to connect the other twenty-four letters that bridge the process. When the mind is renewed by the Spirit, it is evidence that the Spirit of understanding is beginning to operate in us.

I need Your understanding, Holy Spirit. Wash away any disappointment or discouragement that has dulled my heart. Open my eyes so that I can see You clearly. I want Your understanding to flood my heart. Help me to see the treasures hidden in the Word of God. Help me to understand Your ways.

53

Intimacy Through Understanding

Jesus knew the secrets of the hearts of men and women. We see this at work in the story of the woman at the well. He knew her thoughts and the details of her life. I believe the Spirit of knowledge opens us up to knowing God, to knowing His thoughts and His secrets. This was a marker in the life of the Lord. This is not the type of knowledge that "puffs up" (see 1 Cor. 8:1). Rather, it is the "knowing of God." First and foremost, this is connected to intimacy.

God's desire is that we "know Him" instead of "facts." Once we begin to know the Holy Spirit, He begins to share His thoughts and feelings with us. Before He shares secrets with us, He wants us. Before we hear from Him, He wants us to meet Him…or at least to meet Him in the process. Nonetheless, His priority is knowing Him.

Once we encounter the Holy Spirit as a person, we will discover that He has a lot to talk about. However, He will never exchange intimacy for information. For instance, words of knowledge (see 1 Cor. 12:8) should be a byproduct of the knowledge of Him. When John was called into His encounter in the Book of Revelation, he heard, *"Come up here, and I will show you…"* (Rev. 4:1). To make it simple, the Spirit of knowledge leads us into the knowing of God, which opens our hearts to know God's thoughts, which is meant to lead us into a deeper intimacy with God.

> *Thank You, Holy Spirit, that there is not one area of my heart that is hidden from You. You know me better than I know myself. That You are also willing to be fully known by me is astounding. I long to be close to You, to know Your heart, and to understand Your ways. I will quiet my mind and wait to experience Your heart right now. There is nothing I want more than intimacy with You.*

54

Wonderful Counselor

Proverbs 8:14 says, *"Counsel is mine, and sound wisdom: I am understanding; I have strength"* (KJV). Isaiah 9:6 declares, "*... His name shall be called Wonderful Counselor...*" (ESV). The Lord is certainly our counselor. Can you imagine that God is ready to give you advice to help you decide on pivotal issues, to warn you, and to instruct you? To take it a step further, we are invited by the Holy Spirit into the counsel of God. We literally have been given an open door to hear the conversations of God. Just look at Psalm 22.

Jeremiah rebuked the false prophets of Israel for continually releasing false words of prophecy. He repeatedly said, "Repent because the Babylonians are coming. God is going to judge Israel." Over and over, he warned them, with tears in his eyes, to come back to the Lord. And when he would release the word of God to the king and the king's counselors, they were outraged by it. Other prophets stood up and said, "The Babylonians are not coming, we will not be judged. God is going to bless Israel," and Jeremiah rebuked them.

In other words, the false prophets were false because they had not stood in the counsel of the Lord. They had not given God the time to lift their souls. They spoke on their own accord because the Spirit of counsel was not flowing in their lives. Remember, Jesus said, "The Holy Spirit will not speak of Himself, but He will tell us of everything He hears that comes from the Father and the Son" (see John 16:13). As you listen to the Holy Spirit, you are listening to the will of the Father that is administrated by the Son through the voice of the Holy Spirit.

To be clear, to receive the counsel of the Holy Spirit is to receive the counsel of the Godhead. We are literally invited into the plans of God. God has a plan for America. God has a plan for the nations of the world. God has a plan for every stay-at-home mom in the world. He has a plan for your pastor, and He has a plan for your children. He has a plan for everything and everyone, and God wants to share that plan with us. God has a perfect plan for every service, every Bible study, and every family.

I'm so grateful that You are my loving and caring counselor. Forgive me for all the times that I have acted like the false prophets of Israel—not giving You time to show me Heaven's perspective, speaking and acting out of my own limited understanding. I am in awe that I can receive the counsel of the Godhead for my life. Your plans are so trustworthy and so much better than my own.

55

Worship and Wait

When the Spirit of counsel is invited in through a hungry, yielded heart, God begins to speak to us and share His plans with us. This is so precious for many reasons. Can you believe that God is eager to share His dearest and deepest feelings with you, His friend? The Spirit of counsel opens your ears to the Mighty Counselor.

I have learned that it is much easier to join what God is already doing than to attempt to get God to bless what I am doing. Early on in my ministry days, this was a real struggle for me. There was so much that I wanted to see happen in the meetings, and they were all wonderful ambitions. They were all biblical. I would strive and strive, and nothing would happen. I so badly wanted the sick to be healed. I wanted revival with every fiber of my being. I wanted the fire of God to sweep through our meetings. And to be honest, those things rarely happened.

Finally, I realized that instead of trying to twist God's arm, I could simply wait and listen to Him. Once I sensed, saw, heard, or felt what He was doing, I learned simply to yield to that plan. That combination became a combustible reward. The power of God was released in those services. What was once dead quickly came to life. I realized that God had a plan for every moment of every day. Saying "yes" to that plan was the bridge that connected Heaven and earth in the moment. Once that connection took place, I simply had to hold on for the ride.

I'll never forget telling Heidi Baker, "Heidi, I struggled for so many years, and then one day I sensed that Jesus just wanted to walk into our meetings—that if I could figure out a way to allure Him to walk through the services, He would come. So I just began to worship and wait, Heidi, and He came and did everything so much better, so much more powerfully." Heidi looked at me with a smile, and she said, "That's it. Isn't it way better that way?"

I am hungry for Your presence, Holy Spirit. Would You stir up my hunger even more? I am fully yielded to Your will. Search my heart, and reveal to me any area that I have yet to surrender to You. I want to align my will, my heart, and my life with You. I will not try to make You fit my plans; I will worship and wait for You to show me Yours.

56

The Spirit of Might

The Spirit of might is awesome. There are times in our lives where we need breakthrough, we need God to do the impossible. Miracles are a part of our lives as Christians. The Spirit of might is so needed in the Church today, and I believe God wants to pour it out in a huge way.

Might is great strength, force, or power. Deuteronomy 3:24 says, *"O Lord God, thou hast begun to shew thy servant thy greatness, and thy mighty hand: for what God is there in heaven or in earth, that can do according to thy works, and according to thy might?"* (KJV). Let's remember, in our own strength, we have no might. Psalm 24:8 says, *"Who is this King of glory? The Lord strong and mighty, the Lord mighty in battle."* The source of power and might is God

Himself. Job 12:13 declares, *"With Him are wisdom and might..."* (NASB).

Have you ever pondered the incredible victory that Jesus accomplished on the cross and through His resurrection? Just think for a moment about how when Jesus died, He descended into the underworld and took captivity captive. The Bible goes on to say that He embarrassed the devil himself. This side of Jesus is one of my favorites. I love the fact that He's strong and mighty. Can you picture Him down there enforcing His greatness and victory? How about the Jesus who turned over the money tables? Or how about the Jesus who cast out demons with a spoken word?

Jeremiah 32:18–19 says, *"...the Great, the Mighty God, the Lord of hosts, is his name, great in counsel, and mighty in work..."* (KJV). Daniel describes Him this way in Daniel 2:20: *"Blessed be the name of God forever and ever, to whom belong wisdom and might"* (ESV).

> *Thank You, Holy Spirit, that You bring Your power and might into the world. You are stronger than anything I'm facing. I can rest like a child in the strong arms of my Father.*

57

SURRENDER AND HUNGER

To God, everything is done. At the cross, Jesus paid the price for every stubbed toe and every cancerous tumor. He purchased every healing and every miracle for every person that has ever lived. Every allergy and every dead body waiting to be raised, and everything in between, have been paid for by Jesus Himself. Yet the Bible does say in Acts 19:11 that *"God wrought special miracles by the hands of Paul"* (KJV).

When God speaks, it is completed. The question is, how do we walk in and experience what is already in our account? Well, there are many answers, but at the end of the day, I believe surrender and hunger are two of the greatest keys we could ever possess in accessing the Spirit of might, the Holy Spirit Himself.

Samson understood the Spirit of might after running miles carrying a gate to a city. Elijah knew the Spirit of might as he lived on no food for forty days and journeyed, and preached, and ministered. Paul knew the Spirit of might as he shook off a viper that bit him in the hand. Jesus understood the Spirit of might when all were healed in entire cities and villages. Just imagine—Jesus could cast a devil out of somebody in an entirely different city just through the spoken word. This is the Spirit of might in operation. Jesus showed us the Spirit of might when He walked on water and multiplied bread and fish. The Holy Spirit will change you. The Holy Spirit will make you into a real man or woman of God.

There is nothing overwhelming for You, Holy Spirit. Anything that comes against the Kingdom of God has already been defeated by the death and resurrection of Jesus. I can stand in Your victory, today, knowing that Your miraculous interventions are available to me.

58

Our Weakness for His Strength

When you think of the revivalists and the great voice of the healing movement, you think of Oral Roberts laying hands on ten thousand people in one night, many being healed as his hands touched them. Think of Kathryn Kuhlman, this frail, old woman traveling from city to city, preaching her heart out and ministering to the sick. Think of Maria Woodworth-Etter continuing in her ministry after losing five of her children to disease. Some testified that as she would pull into a town, people would fall under the power a mile in each direction. How could this happen? The Holy Spirit, the Spirit of might. He takes your weakness and hides it in Himself. He then uses that weakness as space to fill you with His power.

How badly we need the Spirit of might today! Hospitals are fuller than ever. Nations around the world are waiting to hear the Gospel. Governments need to see miracles. Presidents and prime ministers have sick family members and their money cannot save them, yet they're looking for somebody or something to deliver them. Churches are hungry for the genuine presence of God. Sickness stands and mocks the promises of God. All the while Jesus is waiting for somebody's surrender to carry His touch.

The Holy Spirit is more ready than we could ever be. He's ready to touch the world. What is He looking for? A life that recognizes its own weakness; somebody who says to themselves and to God, "I need You. I may not have much to give You, but if I get You, I get everything. Here I am, Lord. Touch me."

I pray that like Paul in Romans 15:19, many will say of our lives, *"Through mighty signs and wonders, by the power of the Spirit of God...*[we] *have fully preached the gospel of Christ"* (KJV). And so, this is my prayer for you—it's actually a Scripture that I would like to speak over you as you read this: *"Finally, my brethren, be strong in the Lord, and in the power of His might"* (Eph. 6:10).

> *I am so aware of my own weaknesses, Holy Spirit. I need You. I need You to touch every part of my heart and every area of my life. My family needs Your presence, Your restoration, and Your grace. My city needs to see Your transformative power. My nation needs Your intervention, Your wisdom, and Your peace. Here I am, Lord. Touch me.*

59

The Fear of the Lord

"*The fear of the Lord is the beginning of wisdom*" (Prov. 9:10). This implies that without the fear of the Lord, we walk in foolishness and blindness before God. Our eyes are unable to see who He is. It is literally the gateway to the vision of God. The Bible says that Jesus was anointed with the Spirit of the fear of the Lord (see Isa. 11:2). The fear of the Lord is to be simply in awe of God. It is an awe that draws us to the Lord. It is an awe that creates a dependence on the Lord.

The Bible says that those who fear the Lord have lips that are free from deceit (see Ps. 34:13). As Joy Dawson would say, this does not only mean that we tell the truth but that we tell all of the truth all of the time. There are no exaggerations or white lies in the fear of the Lord. It is an awareness that God is always there, always listening, and always watching. It is an absolute obsession with His presence and the understanding that we have His attention.

As we grow in the fear of the Lord, we grow in wisdom. We begin to see the Lord for who He is. That He is alpha and omega. That He is love and fire. A sobriety comes into our lives as we realize that we will give an account for everything done in this body, as Paul said in Second Corinthians 5:10 (see 2 Cor. 5:10).

When the fear of the Lord touches you, you begin to see the absolute holiness of the Lord. I believe this is what happened to John the beloved on the island of Patmos when he saw the resurrected Jesus in Revelation 1. This is why he fell dead at His feet. He saw into the Lord in a way that he had never seen before. This happened on the Mount of Transfiguration when Peter, John, and James were afraid by what they saw: Jesus permeating flashes of lightning from His body, the cloud of the Holy Spirit hovering above them, the fire within the cloud, and the voice of the Father. What a scene as they encountered the fear of the Lord. Moses had this experience on Mount Sinai as he beheld the Ancient of Days, amazed by the fire that engulfed the entire mountain.

Holy Spirit, would You touch me today and give me a fresh revelation of the fear of the Lord? You are so holy, so mighty, so worthy of my awe and praise. I never want to take Your presence for granted or minimize who You are simply because You have made Yourself so accessible to me. Show me Your splendor in a new way.

60

Grace and Truth

As God moves into the scene and expresses Himself, our humanity realizes His absolute greatness. It is in holy experiences like this where we realize that God is everything, that He is pure and holy, and that He is absolute light with no darkness, or shadow, or turning (see James 1:17). While we are incredibly aware of His love for us, we also realize that He holds our breath in His hand and that we are but dust.

To be honest, I want a God whom I fear this way. I want a Jesus who is holy. I love the fact that He has eyes of fire and a rod in His hand. I love the fact that He's righteous and just. Understanding this makes me more amazed at the fact that this amazing God, who has no beginning and no end, would come and die for me. The Holy Spirit gives us the fear of the Lord. In fact, Jesus delighted in the fear of the Lord (see Isa. 11:3).

I'm privileged to minister and have a relationship with many denominations and streams. I have preached to young and old, Baptists and Pentecostals, Catholics and Methodists, and everything in between. There's something that has been concerning me as of late. It is the thought that because of God's amazing grace, we no longer need the fear of the Lord. Proof that grace has touched your life is the presence of the fear of the Lord on your life. The Bible says that grace and truth come through Jesus (see John 1:17). In other words, they literally flow through the person of Jesus. He is the source and the means by which grace and truth come to our lives. Therefore, we should become more and more like Jesus every day if we are experiencing His grace.

The ancient fathers of the Church used to say this about somebody who carried the glory of God: "He has been graced with the Holy Spirit." In other words, grace was not so much a free pass to do whatever you want, but it was the power that bathed and wrapped God's friends in the Holy Spirit. To put it quite simply, if you want to know that grace is flowing and winning in your life, you should be more like Jesus today than you were yesterday.

Thank You, Holy Spirit, that we have the only example of perfect light, absolute holiness, and complete purity in the entire universe. I never want to lose sight of Your truth or of Your empowering grace. Search my heart, Holy Spirit. Is there any area of my life where I have become prideful? I want Your grace to transform me.

61

When No One Is Watching

The fear of the Lord will challenge you. God will test you to see if you, like Jesus, will delight in the fear of the Lord. Charles Spurgeon says, "You are who you are when nobody is watching." In other words, if you want to know the real you, the real you is the one who lives when nobody is watching.

I've had God challenge me so many times in private with what might look like small things—like putting a shopping cart back that's out in the middle of a parking lot, or picking up a piece of garbage, or giving a poor person a few dollars. Sometimes He challenges me to pick up somebody's tab in a restaurant. Maybe you're asking, "What's that got to do with the fear of the Lord?" Everything! When His voice outweighs the opinions of men and your own opinions, you are beginning to walk in the fear of the Lord.

The beauty of this is that God will begin to open up the treasure of wisdom as He sees that we can be trusted with the fear of the Lord. His wisdom is so precious that it must fall into the lives of those who are trustworthy and have shown Him that they value Him above all else. Character carries gifting and revelation. The fear of the Lord forges character in our lives. Without the Holy Spirit it is impossible to have the fear of the Lord, but with Him it is your promise.

I want to stand before You, confident that I have acted with the same integrity in front of people as I have when nobody is watching. Holy Spirit, what is a challenge that You would give me today? Where would You like to stretch my capacity? Keeping this secret with only You, I want to do something today that will continue to forge character within me.

62

Wine and Oil

There's a beautiful story in the Scriptures of a priest who is traveling on a road and on his way he is beaten up, hurt badly, robbed, and who ends up in really bad shape. The first person that goes by decides not to help him, but then a Samaritan comes by, sees him, and the Bible says he does something amazing. He pours wine and oil on his wounds (see Luke 10:25–37).

The Holy Spirit is referred to as wine in the Scriptures. Paul actually makes a comparison by saying, *"Be not drunk with wine… but be filled with the Spirit"* (Eph. 5:18). Wine is interesting because it possesses many qualities that are very similar to those of the Holy Spirit.

You remember the story of the wedding in Cana? It was the setting for Jesus' first miracle. I love this story for so many reasons.

First and foremost, I love it because it involves Jesus. I love anything that involves Him. Secondly, it's a beautiful picture of His relationship with His mother and of the beautiful, natural nature of Jesus. He was not too spiritual to attend a wedding and celebrate with those who are celebrating.

Mary comes to the Lord because there is a problem at the wedding. They had run out of wine. And so, the master of the ceremony was a bit stressed. Mary came to the Lord and told Him. After dialoguing with Mary and after a little back-and-forth with His mother, Jesus gave direction, and He told the servants, "Fill up the vessels with water" (see John 2:7). And they filled up the vessels with water, and by the power of the Holy Spirit, that water was turned into wine. Everyone began to drink after the miracle took place. And the people said, "You have saved the best wine for last. Typically, the best wine is first, but you saved the best for last" (see John 2:10).

Isn't this a picture of the Holy Spirit in so many different ways? It is an especially beautiful picture of the way of the Holy Spirit. As amazing as Pentecost was, for instance, He promises that the latter will be greater than the former—that the rain, that the glory of the latter house would be greater than that of the former house (see Hag. 2:9).

Holy Spirit, You look forward. You are not bound by time. I long to experience the wine of the Spirit. You promise that the latter will be greater than the former. I stand on that promise today.

63

Cleansing Joy

The wine in the story of the Good Samaritan was used *to disinfect and to bring healing to the wounds of the priest who was hurt so badly.* The oil would cover and protect the wound and cause the wound to begin closing. It would keep infection from setting in long term. It would become a calming agent to the wound. But the initial application would have been the wine because wine disinfects.

Now, this is a picture of the blood of Jesus, no doubt, but it is also a picture of the wine of the Holy Spirit and His work. The Holy Spirit not only protects us and empowers us, but He also disinfects us. He is actually the One who brings and carries the benefits of the blood of Jesus to our lives. That's what the Bible teaches—that the blessings of Abraham have come to us by the

Spirit (see Gal. 3:14). In fact, the blood and the Spirit and water, the Bible says, work together; they bear witness in Heaven and on earth (see 1 John 5:8). It is the same today. The Holy Spirit and the power of the blood, they work in perfect harmony. The Bible says that it was through the blood of Jesus that the Holy Spirit raised Jesus from the dead (see Heb. 13:20).

Next, when wine is consumed in the Spirit and we are filled with the Spirit, we experience what David called "an intoxication." This is full of joy, full of peace. There is a holy inebriation that comes to those who are constantly beholding the Lord. The early saints of old talked about this. The 120 in the upper room on the day of Pentecost were called drunkards because of the work of the Holy Spirit. Some believe that this is because they spoke in tongues, but that is not the case. Let me ask you a simple question: If your friend, who spoke perfect English and only perfect English, all of a sudden began to speak perfect Portuguese, would you attribute that to drinking alcohol? No. You would say, "You're a genius."

So why were they called drunkards? It was because of the effect that the Holy Spirit was having on them, the joy that He was producing in their souls, the way that they were declaring the Word of the Lord in the native tongues of all who were listening. The wine of Heaven brings a happiness and a peace that nothing else can. I believe that this is one of the gifts from the Lord that helps us experience the following Scripture: "We are in the world but not of the world" (see John 17:16). In other words, our bodies are planted here on earth. Our minds are dealing with both worlds; but deep in our spirit, the new wine of Heaven begins to flow, and we receive this heavenly drink that causes us to lose sight of all that holds us. All the fear and all the worry that the world offers begin to dissipate, and we begin to live a true heavenly life.

Pour out the wine of heaven over me, Holy Spirit. I open up my heart to Your cleansing. Wash away anything that is not of You, anything that is bringing death and decay into my life. And then fill me with Your overwhelming joy! I want to experience Your joy as more real than any challenges I'm facing. I want to live a heavenly life in You.

64

Holy Spirit Fire

The Holy Spirit is so vast. There are so many facets to His nature. Yes, He's one. The Bible says, "He came as a dove," but He is not a dove. He appeared as a fire but was not a bush. He is spoken about as being a wind, but there is so much more to Him than being a wind. The point is this: These beautiful pictures are descriptions of His nature, and He wants you to get to know Him.

Let's talk about the Holy Spirit as fire. John the Baptist said, "There's one coming after me who will baptize you in the Holy Spirit and fire, whose sandals I am not worthy to unloose" (see Matt. 3:11; Luke 3:16). Again, we see in Exodus chapter 3 that Moses encounters a bush that would not burn, and from that bush there was a fire. As the children of Israel walked through the wilderness for forty years, a pillar of fire went before them and led them through the dark night of their journey to the Promised Land. That fire was not only a light but also a warmth that would protect them, keep predators away, and let the nations of the world know that although they were in the wilderness, they still belonged to God. He was their light and their heat.

When Moses dedicated the tabernacle, God showed His approval by descending as fire on the altar, and that fire never went out. Solomon fulfilled the dream of his father and through the wisdom of God built the temple and followed the blueprint that David handed down to him. After assembling Israel, the Levites, the musicians, the beautiful choir, the different artifacts, and the pieces of the holy temple, Solomon dedicated it to the Lord, and the Lord appeared, descended as fire, and consumed the sacrifice.

You are so gracious to reveal Yourself in ways that our minds can comprehend, Holy Spirit. I want to understand more and more of who You are, what You're like, and how You manifest in the world. Will You show me when You've been like a pillar of fire in my life—protecting and guiding me? Will You show me when You've been like the consuming fire—acknowledging and blessing my sacrifice?

65

Consuming Fire

"One's coming after me who will baptize you in the Holy Spirit and fire" (see Matt. 3:11; Luke 3:16). Again, the Bible says, *"Our God is a consuming fire"* (Heb. 12:29). It's interesting that John chose to introduce Jesus as the baptizer in the Holy Spirit and fire while John was baptizing people himself in water. It was the perfect opportunity to give an illustrated sermon.

In every baptism, there are a few things we need to understand regarding God's way of baptizing. There is the baptizer, there is the baptizee, there is the element that we're baptized into, and then there is the result or fruit of the baptism. In John's baptism, John was the baptizer, the people that came to him were the baptizees, the element was water, and the fruit of that baptism was repentance. This is why John said that we were to show the fruit of repentance to work the works of repentance (see Matt. 3:8). In the baptism of the Holy Spirit and fire, the baptizer is Jesus, the baptizees are you and me, the element is the Holy Spirit and fire, and the fruit is this: "You will become witnesses unto Me" (see Acts 1:8).

So, as John stood at the banks and took people who came to him and plunged them into the waters of the Jordan, so Jesus takes us as we come to Him and plunges us into the depths of the river of God, a river of presence and fire. We literally come out dripping with the very substance of God Himself.

Now, God is not just a flame. He is not a tiny little candle hoping to be seen. No, the Lord is a real fire. To be even more precise, He is a certain type of fire: He is a consuming fire. The fire of the Holy Spirit protects us, warms us, illuminates us, but it also burns up all that is in us that is not of God. In other words, when the Holy Spirit is done burning in us, only He and His presence remain.

We need fire again. We need real Holy Spirit fire. Our generation is tired of sitting through services that are perfectly planned, perfectly calm, perfectly directed by men and women, yet leave the sinner a sinner, leave the backslider backslidden, and leave those sick and suffering in their disease. We need real fire again.

I want to be baptized again, in the fire of Your presence. I want anything that is not of You to be burned up and discarded. I long to emerge from Your presence, dripping with You, revealing Your heart to a hungry world. I am crying out for more of You, Holy Spirit. Come and fill me again today.

66

HERE TO SERVE

I believe in impartation. I believe in serving and honoring those who have gone before us. This is a precious and vital truth in growing in the Lord and influence in the earth. I believe in surrounding ourselves with men and women who have achieved more and experienced more in the Lord than we have. I have many of those people in my own life. While I do believe that mantles can be transferred and that impartation can take place, I have also seen many people take their eyes off Jesus because they're so focused on a man's mantle.

Let's have a look at the life of Jesus and see the mantle that He chose. The Bible says that on the night He was betrayed, He took the cup and shared the Last Supper with His disciples. When they were through celebrating the Passover, the Scripture says that Jesus took off His cloak, laid it down, took a rag, and girded Himself with it (see John 13:4). This is incredibly powerful language.

In those days, what you wore told the world who you were and what you did. Your clothing was a picture of your status in society. Jesus was a rabbi; therefore, He wore a rabbi's clothing. But here in this holy moment, He takes His garment off and wears a rag. This is amazing. He was not merely saying, "I am here to serve and to wash feet," though that is amazing in itself. He was saying, "I am here to be a servant." You see, being and doing something once are completely different. Jesus took off His mantle of honor, took on the nature of a servant, and began to wash the feet of His disciples.

The Lord of my life took off His garment and tied a rag around Himself. The Creator of the universe bent down and tenderly washed the dirty feet of His creation. I am humbled and in awe of You, Jesus. Holy Spirit, show me how I can emulate His servant's heart. What is one, tangible act of service I can offer someone today?

67

The Mantle of the Cross

What was the next mantle that Jesus sought? I would venture to say you've never heard what you're about to read. Jesus endured the cross with joy and put the cross on His back as a mantle. He wore a mantle of wood—a mantle that marked Him as a reject of society and as a criminal. We see many miracles, and I will never shortchange that. But more than any mantle of man that you need, we all need to wear the mantle of the cross.

This is a heavy mantle. It's a mantle whose weight you feel. It is a holy weight that marks you before the heavens and the world, that notifies demonic powers that you are following the path of Jesus. As Madame Guyon said, "God gives us the cross, and the cross gives us God." When you say, "Jesus, I will carry my cross" and obey His command that *"if any man will come after me, let him deny himself, and take up his cross daily, and follow me"* (Luke 9:23 KJV), the moment you do that—the moment you deny self and put a cross on your back—every devil in hell will know something: *This man belongs to God.* It's a clear announcement to the unseen world that you are not your own.

What we often forget to realize is that once that cross is embedded into your nature and you wear it gladly, it becomes more than a cross. It becomes an altar. That's right, the cross is an altar. That's why the altar of sacrifice in the tabernacle was in the shape of a cross. It's because instead of a lamb being slaughtered every day, one day the Lamb of God would be slaughtered on that cross. And so, the cross is Heaven's altar. Instead of the blood of animals, the blood of Jesus runs down that cross.

Do you remember what falls on the altar? Can you remember how God gives His "amen" upon an altar? It's by sending fire. And so, as you place the cross on your back, it becomes a magnet for the fire of the Holy Spirit.

Holy Spirit, help me to follow the path of Jesus. I have come to die to every ounce of control, self-preservation, manipulation, and fear. I surrender it all to You, and I pick up the cross with a sober joy. I belong to God. Let my life become an altar that would draw Your fiery presence, Holy Spirit.

68

Authentic Oil

My wife, Jessica, is really into health. I must say, so am I. For example, Jessica never puts the synthetic bug spray on our kids. We love to be outdoors. Playing golf and fishing are our favorite pastimes. In Florida, bugs are a big deal. They are literally everywhere. The mosquitoes down here do a lot more than fly by. They bite you and bite you again. They have a way of making you want to go crazy. So, we have to lather ourselves with bug spray. We use a healthy, organic alternative. I have to admit, it does work. There is only one issue: it leaves you feeling a little oily. Oil is the base substance for the bug sprays we use. While the oily spray does repel most of the bugs, some are so committed to sucking our blood that they fly straight into the oil. Guess what? They die when they land.

This is so much like the anointing of the Holy Spirit on our lives. Yes, there are many counterfeit alternatives out there. There are actually church conferences and books out there that teach you how to grow your ministry systematically but don't mention a relationship with the Holy Spirit. They will tell you how your services should be scheduled, but they don't reference bathing in the oil of God so that He can flow through you in the meeting. Yes, just as there are many synthetic bug sprays out there that work in the short term but cause harm in the long term, there are synthetic solutions to ministry.

We must choose daily to contend for the authentic life in the Holy Spirit, which Jesus modeled for us. Success is loving Jesus, not growing in numbers. Growth should be a byproduct of genuine union with the Holy Spirit. Reject the synthetic, man-made methods by yielding to God's voice in your life.

Just as the genuine oil protects me and my children from bugs, so the Holy Spirit protects us from the powers of hell. In the bug repellant, it is the smell of the oil and the spices that keeps the bugs away. The same is true in the spiritual life. It is the fragrance of Jesus in the oil of the Spirit that repels the attacks of the enemy. The devil literally hates the presence of the Holy Spirit. However, if an attack does get through to us (just as there are bugs that occasionally reach our skin despite the natural bug spray), the Holy Spirit—Pure Oil—protects us.

I want to be dripping with the authentic oil of Your presence, Holy Spirit. Today I remember that Your presence covers me. Your oil protects me. I will draw close to You.

69

Oil of Protection

Did you know that David was anointed three times: once as a shepherd boy (possibly at the age of twelve) so that he could kill Goliath, another time as king of Judah, and lastly as king of Israel. David was very familiar with the precious oil—the presence of the Holy Spirit. His first anointing, given by Samuel while he tended to his sheep, would change his life forever. His private battle-tested skills would now go public and take center stage before all of Israel. He knew the effect that the oil had on his life. Of course he sensed something different on him.

Who was it that gave David the boldness to challenge Goliath before two nations? Where did the certainty come from that he would not only kill Goliath, but also cut off Goliath's head and even kill Goliath's brothers? Remember, he took five smooth stones from the brook. Goliath had four brothers, and God never does anything by chance. What carried that rock directly into Goliath's forehead? Was David really that good? The answer to all of the above is the presence of the Spirit that rested on David once the oil was poured on him by Samuel, God's prophet.

After years of testing and turmoil, David would eventually be king of Judah and Israel. Yet, David failed—many times and in many ways. He was an adulterer, a murderer, a horrible friend, a deceiver, prideful, self-exalting, and greedy. In fact, in comparison to the people who often receive our scorn, David was the worst offender. Did God punish David? Yes, He did. He punished him harshly, but He didn't throw him away. Why? First and foremost, because David repented. It was also because he wore the oil. The oil reminded God that David was the Lord's and that one day, the Eternal King would take His eternal throne as the offspring of David.

Given David's many failures, should we erase his successes and heart for the Lord? Should we eliminate First and Second Samuel eternally from the Scriptures? How about the Book of Psalms? What about Jesus' title as Son of David? Of course not! Why must David remain honored before us? It's because God chose him. God raised him up. God poured His oil on him. If he is good enough for God, he should be good enough for us.

When you honor what is of God in the lives of people, you honor Him. When we honor the Holy Spirit, He entrusts us with more of His presence.

Your anointing protects and covers. It identifies the one anointed as belonging to You forever. Forgive me, Holy Spirit, for any time that I have scorned or dishonored one of Your anointed, even if it was only in my heart. If there is someone who has come to mind, whose choices have offended me, would You show me what You love about that person? What part of Your heart have You placed within them?

70

ENCOUNTERING HIM

In 2016, I was privileged to speak to hundreds of students in Pasadena, California. As I flew home from California to Orlando, I began to think about God's calling on my life. As I began to contemplate my assignment, I realized that it was very simple: to preach Jesus and to lead people to a genuine encounter with the reality of His presence. The reality of His presence on earth is the Holy Spirit. I believe in my heart that I am nothing more than a follower of Jesus who leads people into a great and loving collision with the person of Jesus Himself.

I must say, it deeply saddens me when I hear leaders say that it doesn't matter what you feel and that we don't need God to touch us, we only need to believe the Bible. The problem with that thought process is that it is through the Bible that God wants to touch us. Did you know that the Bible is not about the Bible? Did you know that Scriptures are not about Scriptures?

You're probably experiencing a bit of a shock right now as you read this, but before you cast your opinion, let me say that the Bible is the inspired Word of God. The Bible is the heartbeat of God on paper. The Scriptures are alive. The Scriptures are the revealed will of God, and the living Scriptures plus the presence of the Spirit equal a revelation of Jesus, who is the face of the Father. I would say I read my Bible as much or more than anyone I know. I love the Scriptures, and I love my physical copy of the Bible. It's been with me for years, and I've cried while reading it. To me, the Bible is much more than a book. It's an experience. Did you know that the church fathers called the Holy Scriptures "the book of experience"? But they were after something more. They were after the Person of the Bible.

God gave us the Bible to bring us to Himself. And so, the Scriptures should lead us to the One who wrote them. After all, they do reveal His heart and His mind to us. Again, the Scriptures are 100 percent divine and true from Genesis to Revelation. I am only making the point that there are many who own and read their Bibles who do not believe that Jesus is the Son of God. The bottom line is this: God gave us the Holy Scriptures so that we would meet Him.

You are the reality of Jesus' presence on the earth, Holy Spirit. Everything that I do—whether it would be called spiritual or not—revolves around encountering You, learning from You, revealing You to the world. Thank You for Your Word. Thank You that it is tangible proof that You want to be known by me. Where would You have me read in the Scriptures today? I want to meet You there.

71

HE IS REAL

If there is anything I would want you to experience and understand, it would be this: how literal and real the person of the Holy Spirit is. No, He's not a concept. He's a real person. When you met your husband or your wife, you longed to get closer with time. He wants the same. He's not interested in a long-distance relationship that is merely full of lifeless information or historical facts. He wants to touch you. The Lord is looking to get face to face with you and kiss you. *"Let him kiss me with the kisses of his mouth..."* (Song of Sol. 1:2). This shows the posture of heart that we should all have. We want God to kiss us. We don't want just one kiss; we want kisses.

What does it take to be kissed by God? Well, it means to be face to face with Him. It means to stare into His eyes of fire—and that fire is the Holy Spirit Himself. Jesus has eyes of fire because He's full of the Spirit. Adam breathed in the Lord's breath, and we do the same as we look at Jesus and worship Him. This is impossible from far away, and it is equally impossible without touch.

Jesus knew the touch of the Spirit. Do you remember what happened while Jesus was on His way to raise that dead girl, the daughter of Jairus? As He was walking through the village, a woman with the issue of blood, weak and broken, crawled through the crowd just to get to Jesus. She had spent all her money on doctors. She was looked at by the entire community as being unclean. This poor woman, who some think was named Lydia, could not worship with the rest of her community or leave her home. She was rejected by society and completely broken, and her only hope came walking down the street. When she got to Jesus, she touched Him. Instantly, Jesus stopped in His tracks. He said, "Who touched Me?"

A disciple said, "Lord, what do You mean who touched You? Everyone's touching You."

He said, "No, someone touched Me. I felt power leave Me. I felt virtue leave Me." And He looked down and saw that woman, and she was healed (see Luke 8:43–48). Jesus was so sensitive to the activity of the Holy Spirit in His life that He could literally feel the power of God leave Him. Life in the Spirit is incredibly touch oriented.

Holy Spirit, I want to know what Your presence feels like. I want to see You move in my life. Thank You that You have given me so many different ways to experience Your presence. Open the eyes of my heart to all the ways that it is possible to know You.

72

Waiting in His Presence

I'm often asked, "Michael, how can I walk in the Spirit so that I can love Jesus?" What do you do when you pray? Tell me what your quiet time looks like. "I want to be closer with God." Well, I can't tell you exactly how you should commune with the Lord. I can offer you in the simplest way possible a description of how I spend time with God. Again, we all have our own walk with the Lord, and He deals differently with each of us. Yet the Scriptures do tell us that there are general and beautiful ways by which we all can enjoy His presence.

It's usually early in the morning before the sun is up. Before I open my eyes, I feel a pull deep within my heart. The pull is constant, strong, but not rude. It's heavy, but not burdensome. It seems to have hooks deep within my heart. Those hooks are attached to cords, as described in the following Scripture: "He draws me with cords of love" (see Hos. 11:4). This pull has a voice. The voice is very loving, and it's simple too. It says, "Michael, I'm here. Get up; I want to be with you. It's time to spend time together." Usually, a few minutes goes by until I can muster the strength to get up out of my bed, but I notice that before I'm fully awake, He's already tugging. So, I sit up and roll out of the bed as quietly as possible so that I don't wake up my wife. I grab a quick coffee to wake up, and I head to my prayer room. Jesus said in Matthew chapter 6, "When you pray, close the door," and so I simply obey (see Matt. 6:6). I close the door, grab my Bible, and usually just take a seat.

Before I begin to speak or say anything, I simply sit there. You say, "What do you do when you sit there?" Nothing… I take a deep breath, clear my mind. There are mornings where I'll whisper words of love and adoration to the Lord. It might sound something like this: "Jesus, You're beautiful. You're awesome. You're loving. You're kind. I love You. Thank You for waking me up this morning. Here I am. I worship You." And then, I wait some more. Why am I waiting? I'm not necessarily waiting for God to come, but I am waiting in His presence to be quickened by Him.

You see, Saint Augustine said that he spent years looking for God without while the entire time God was within. As I become still and release the cares of the world and just do nothing because I am fully dependent on Him, I will eventually sense the quickening of the Holy Spirit. Sometimes I physically feel it on my body. Sometimes I sense an instant connection with the activity of the Spirit. Sometimes He becomes very real and faith is born.

Regardless, I do nothing until He quickens me. It's in that moment that I begin to praise Him.

> *Holy Spirit, thank You for Your love. Engaging with You isn't tedious or complicated. I can come to You each day, quieting my heart and focusing my mind on Your goodness. Today, I sit before You, grateful for who You are, waiting in Your presence.*

73

One Desire

David said, *"Be still, and know that I am God..."* (Ps. 46:10). The knowledge of God comes in this deep stillness as we wait upon the Lord. Knowledge of God means to know God, not to know about Him. It's in this place of waiting upon Him that you discover His person, His qualities, His likes, and His dislikes. So, when I spend time with God, I wait. How long? It just depends. I'm not waiting on the clock. I am waiting on the Person.

Once I feel that quickening, I then begin to open my mouth and praise the Lord. I give Him glory because He's amazing. I might say something like, "Jesus, You're God Almighty. You've been crucified and raised, and You're seated on the throne. You are the Victorious One. You've defeated death. You're amazing." Sometimes I'll go through His works and His acts in the Scriptures, and when I begin to praise the Lord, I'll sense the reality of His Kingdom in the moment. What do I mean by that? His presence—the presence of the Spirit—begins to rule over me. He overshadows my weakness. He overshadows my fallen desires. And the Kingdom that is within me begins to rule and reign.

From then on, I just follow His lead. I've learned to let the Holy Spirit be my teacher in my quiet time. He might say, "Open your Bible." He might say, "Wait again." He might say, "Sing to Me in the Spirit. Sing to Me an old hymn." Whatever He says, I try to lovingly obey. I've found that it's in that moment that my desires become one with His. So, what I desire, I simply yield to. If I desire to read the Scriptures, I follow that. If I desire to do nothing, I follow that.

There comes a time, when I'm with the Lord, when every desire but a desire for Him dies. That can usually take a while. Once I get to the place where I have one desire, and that is Jesus, I know I'm entering a deep place in the Holy Spirit. It is in this place that your body literally cries out for the presence of God to fill and touch it.

I will not be impatient, Holy Spirit. Still my heart until I become aware of Your presence. I will praise Your name. I will remember the ways that You have guided me, protected me, and intervened on my behalf. Fill me with the awareness of Your Kingdom, Holy Spirit. You are my one desire. I yield completely to You.

74

Wave After Wave

"*My flesh longeth for thee in a dry and thirsty land, where no water is*" (Ps. 63:1 KJV). I do not believe that we are called to live in dryness. Jesus paid a price for our continual fellowship with the Lord. If we ever do suffer distance from the Lord, it's never the Lord's fault. But David wanted more, and he came to the place where he wanted his body to experience the life-giving water of the Spirit.

It's in these times of prayer that I feel completely overwhelmed with His presence. But the language does not become complicated; in fact, it becomes simpler. In that moment, I am not a preacher. I am simply a child of God. And so, my language becomes more singular, more childlike, more basic. You might hear something like this: "Jesus, I love You. Jesus, I need You. You are beautiful." Or you might hear, "Holy Spirit, fill me." Sometimes my heart cries, "I just want You." Then I wait some more and enjoy His beautiful presence. It seems to come like wave after wave after wave. There are spikes, there are peaks, and there are valleys. And so, in the valleys, I wait for Him to sweep through again. In the peaks, I enjoy Him. Once He quickens me, I can share intimate, loving language that ministers back to Him. At the end of the day, I want Him to smile.

Even our prayer time ends with His joy. He receives joy when we receive His joy, but in my heart I want Him to be full of joy when our time is through. You might ask, "When do you stop?" The Scriptures explain this beautifully. In Song of Solomon 8:4, the Bible says, "*...Do not stir up nor awaken love until it pleases.*" I wait until the Lord is through with me, and when I feel that release, I am done. I must say as a comical side note, He's yet to kick me out of the secret place because He's through with me. If I were to spend three hours there, it would seem like He wanted four. If I were to spend eight, it would seem like He wanted nine. If I were to spend my entire day, it would seem like He wanted another. That is how He keeps us coming.

I refuse to be satisfied with a dry, barren life. I know that is not what You intended for me, Holy Spirit. I long to be like David, always wanting more of Your life-giving presence. I will come before You with all boldness, confident that You want to pour out on me even more than I know to ask for. I want You to smile, Holy Spirit.

75

Dependent on the Spirit

And John bore witness saying, "I saw the Spirit descending from heaven like a dove, and He remained upon Him" (John 1:32).

Yes, Jesus is the Son of God. There is absolutely no doubt about that. But even He waited on the Holy Ghost to descend on Him before beginning His ministry. Here's a question we all need to ask ourselves, whether we are Evangelicals, Pentecostals, Charismatics, Baptists, Methodists, Catholics, or Orthodox Christians: If Jesus did not think that the coming of the Spirit upon Him and us was so necessary, why would He wait thirty years to do anything until the Holy Spirit actually came upon Him tangibly? If anyone could've depended on knowledge, experience, and wisdom to follow God, it was Jesus.

Certainly, He has a pretty amazing resume. I mean, after all, according to John 1, He is the creator of everything. The Bible says, *"All things were made by him; and without him was not any thing made that was made"* (John 1:3 KJV). We know that Jesus is eternal. The Scripture says, *"In the beginning was the Word, and the Word was with God..."* (John 1:1). He is all consuming, and everything lives in Him. Colossians 1 says, *"...in Him all things consist"* (Col. 1:17). On top of that, He holds all things together. Hebrews tells us, "He holds all things together by the word of His power" (see Heb. 1:3).

I think it's safe to say that Jesus has a pretty amazing resume and is qualified to be in the ministry, but even Jesus refused to do anything on His own. So how much more should we depend on the Spirit! Why don't you ask the Lord now to overwhelm you with His precious presence?

> *Jesus is my perfect model for all things in life. If He needed You, Holy Spirit, then I definitely do not want to do anything without You. I am joyfully dependent on You. I bring every impossibility that I'm facing, and I lay them down at Your feet.*

76

THROUGH THE SPIRIT

"He *through the Holy Spirit had given commandments to the apostles whom He had chosen*" (Acts 1:2). Do you see four incredible words in that verse? *Through the Holy Spirit.*

Jesus has been raised from the dead as the first fruit. There He was, with wounds in His hands, feet, and side, in a glorious resurrected state, sitting with His disciples. They decided to have a Bible study. Can you imagine having a Bible study with the glorified Son of God? But Jesus refused to have even a mere Bible study unless it was through the Holy Spirit. We have to understand that it is only through the Holy Spirit that we have any connection to the Lord and any ability to reveal Him to others.

So, if the perfect resurrected and victorious Christ depended on the Spirit, my question to you is simply this: How much more do we, as frail humans, need the Spirit in our lives? You see, the presence and power of the Spirit trumps every method and plan. And He will take every weakness and hole in our lives and fill it with His presence. That is why the Bible says, *"Let the weak say, 'I am strong'"* (Joel 3:10).

It is not a sin to be weak. In fact, our weakness, once handed to the Lord, becomes a mighty strength to be reckoned with. He takes those who are not qualified and qualifies them with the anointing of the Spirit. And so, today He looks around and searches the world through and through, not for perfect people, but for people who know they need Him.

> *I know that I need You, Holy Spirit, but I also know that there are areas of my life where I slip back into self-sufficiency. I fall into the trap of thinking I have to come up with solutions all on my own. Will You expose those areas in my life right now, Holy Spirit? Will You show me any area where I am relying on my own strength rather than depending on You?*

77

Willing Vessels

My favorite preacher in history is Kathryn Kuhlman. As I watch video recordings of her ministering, I'm blown away by the tenderness with which she ministered and the dependence that she had on the Holy Spirit. I can hear her words today: "Please don't grieve Him. Don't grieve the Holy Spirit. He is all I've got." That's dependency, and that's why God chose to use her. God is drawn to people who do not believe that they are capable to do His work with their own ability, and few in modern times exemplified that quality more than Kathryn Kuhlman. She was convinced of her inability, and because of that, she yielded to God's ability. One of my favorite quotes from Miss Kuhlman is this: "He doesn't choose golden vessels. He doesn't choose silver vessels. He chooses willing vessels."

I've met so many who have shied away from the ways of the Holy Spirit because of fear. They become nervous because of things they've seen or heard regarding life in the Spirit. Some of the examples they cite are actually the work of the Holy Spirit, some are not, but it would be foolish to throw out all the Holy Spirit is simply because a few have misrepresented Him.

The Holy Spirit is not owned by Pentecostals or Charismatics. In fact, He is a person whom we receive but do not own. How can a human own God? I want to say clearly that no denomination has exclusive rights to the person of the Holy Spirit. All Christians have the Holy Spirit living on the inside of them. Jesus breathed on His disciples and said, *"Receive the Holy Spirit"* (John 20:22). This was the moment of their conversion. I've met Orthodox priests, Lutheran pastors, Baptist ministers, and Catholic priests who have all been walking in a flourishing, vibrant, and powerful relationship with the Holy Spirit.

Jesus, I'm hungry for You, I need Your presence. Holy Spirit, You are the presence of Jesus. I am not qualified to change the world in my own strength, but if You touch me, I can. I want to know You with everything in me. I want to meet You. I want to be Your friend.

78

Look at Him

I just preached in a Catholic conference in Toulon, France, that was led by a Catholic priest named Jean-Michel. The tent in which it was held was the former tent of John II. There were nuns and priests sitting in the crowd. A priest even got healed as I began to worship the Lord and minister to the sick. These Catholics were glowing with the Holy Spirit.

It might surprise you to know that before the Charismatic Renewal there were no Charismatics by name. The Charismatic movement did not start with Charismatics; it started with two hungry priests crying out to the Lord for a miracle. That outpouring that happened initially spread to the Assemblies of God and filtered into all denominations and shook the world, and we are still riding that wave today. The point is this: The Holy Spirit is not intimidated by our boundaries, yet He will never force Himself on our lives.

I encourage you get to know the Holy Spirit for yourself. Don't let how others have treated Him cause you to reject Him. Regardless of what some have made the experience of walking with the Holy Spirit, use Jesus' life alone as your example and you will find that the Holy Spirit is beautiful, tender, powerful, and sacred. Besides the countless miracles that Jesus performed, did you know that it was the Holy Spirit who raised Jesus from the dead? *"And He was shown to be the Son of God when He was raised from the dead by the power of the Holy Spirit. He is Jesus Christ our Lord"* (Rom. 1:4 NLT). There would have been no resurrection without the Holy Spirit.

So don't worry about what you've seen or heard; just look at Him. Look at Jesus as your example. Look straight into His eyes of fire. Why are His eyes afire? Because the Holy Spirit is fire within Him and around Him. As you look to Jesus regarding the Holy Spirit, all of your fear will disappear. You can trust Him today.

Holy Spirit, help me to dismantle any box that I've unconsciously put You in because of other people's experiences or offense. I don't want to merely know You through other people—even the best of teachers. I want to know the real You for myself. You have made every good thing in my life possible. You are perfectly good, perfectly faithful, perfectly holy.

79

UNDIGNIFIED

I can remember telling others and myself that I will never act in certain ways even if the power of God touches me. My framework was broader than most, but now, after years of getting to know the Lord, I have found that I was incredibly narrow-minded. I was okay with people being saved, healed, filled with the Holy Spirit, prophesying, speaking in tongues, and, of course, falling down. I grew up around people being slain in the Holy Spirit, and that began happening in all of my meetings; but I said to myself, "That is I as far as I want to go. I'm not going any further."

Well, God had many experiences up His sleeve just to prove to me that He is not the God of my box; He's the God of the universe. He's the infinite God who can do whatever He pleases, and if we give Him our lives, He may just shock us by how He touches us.

Just look at David. The Holy Spirit comes upon Him as he celebrates the entry of the ark into Jerusalem, and he begins to dance uncontrollably. And his wife, the daughter of Saul, who was used to the old way, the old regime, ridiculed him (see 2 Sam. 6:14–16). And this happens today as we give our lives over to Him. We may just be a little more undignified than we are comfortable with, and very likely more undignified than others are comfortable with.

We never want to tell God how He can and cannot do things. Just trust the Lord. Don't worry about how He touches you. Don't tell Him He can or cannot do His work in your life unless it's by your standard. He is a faithful Shepherd.

Holy Spirit, is there any way that I have limited You working in my life? Please show me right now if I have resisted You because of my own pride, control, or fear of man. I want to be stripped of anything that hinders You. I will not quench Your presence in my life.

80

His Presence and Power

Have you ever been in a meeting where power is flowing but there is no beauty in the air? No moisture on the words of the person who's speaking? The name of Jesus is not being exalted? Perhaps somebody's giving a prophetic word, sharing details about a person's life and past, but nothing in your heart burns. You don't long to spend more time with Jesus after you hear him or her speak. People may even be healed, but you have no desire to come back the next day. Have you ever asked yourself what brings people to us who are not sick and are born again? It's the presence of God. Oftentimes, we don't understand the difference between God's power and God's presence. God's power sets the captives free. God's power destroys the works of the devil. God's presence helps me fellowship with the Lord.

When Jesus breathed upon the disciples and said, *"Receive the Holy Spirt,"* the Holy Spirit began to live inside of them (John 20:22). In that moment, they became the temple of the Holy Ghost. No matter where they went or who they were with, they carried the presence of the Lord on the inside of them. This is what it means to be born again. As the glory of God lives in the Holy of Holies, in the tabernacle in the wilderness, our bodies have now become tabernacles for the Holy Spirit. This is a beautiful and holy gift, the greatest gift we could ever receive—the indwelling Spirit of God. This is the presence of God in our hearts.

When the storms are raging around us, there is always peace within, and we are always able to retreat into that beautiful tabernacle that is our heart. And as Jesus said, Heaven is within us (see Luke 17:21). This is why Jesus calmed the storm as He slept during the storm. Yes, there was a storm around Him, but within Him there was perfect peace because His peace was not ruled by what went on around Him. He affected what went on around Him through the presence of God within Him. This is how we are to live.

Dear Jesus, I know that You slept in the storm, so I know that I can have peace no matter what I am facing. Your presence within me is more powerful than anything that surrounds me.

81

His Power Flows From His Presence

Are you stressed? Do you have anxiety? Do you feel like the world around you controls you? This could be because you don't know how to find the Lord's presence. Or should I say it this way: You don't know *where* to find the Lord's presence. It is within you. What an advantage we have! We literally carry the Kingdom of God within us who is the King Himself.

I have found that the beauty of the Lord is found in His presence. During ministry, if my gift is manifesting more predominantly than His presence, then I will draw people to my gift instead of the presence. Remember, the power of God upon us sets people free around us. The presence of God within us is the key to our personal fellowship with the Lord.

Let's remember a truth and never forget it: the power flows from the presence of God. The presence of God does not find its origin in the power of God. The power of God flows from Him, and He is His presence. Habakkuk says it this way:

> *Lord, I have heard the report about You and I fear. O Lord, revive Your work in the midst of the years, in the midst of the years make it known; in wrath remember mercy. God comes from Teman, and the Holy One from Mount Paran. Selah. His splendor covers the heavens, and the earth is full of His praise. His radiance is like the sunlight; He has rays flashing from His hand, and there is the hiding of His power* (Hab. 3:2–4 NASB).

The hiding of His power comes from His person. It comes from Him. *"His radiance is like the sunlight,"* verse 4 says. *"He has rays flashing from His hand, and there is the hiding of His power"* (Hab. 3:4 NASB). So many people want power, yet they've never gone to the Lord of power and discovered Him. Let's remember that the presence of the Lord is the Lord Himself.

So, when the Lord breathed on those disciples, they received His indwelling presence. This was enough for them to fellowship with Him every day at any moment. Today, if you know Jesus, you carry the presence of the Lord. He has promised to never leave us or forsake us, even until the end of the age (see Heb. 13:5).

> *Thank You, Holy Spirit, that I don't have to create enough faith to produce power. I don't have to work for You to move in miracles. I don't have to show off my gifting for*

Your anointing to be present. You want Your power to flow through me to the world, but Your power comes from Your presence. Teach me to focus on and love You.

82

Ye Shall Receive Power

"Y*e shall receive power, after that the Holy Ghost is come upon you...*" (Acts 1:8 KJV). Remember that Jesus is speaking to the same disciples that He spoke to when He breathed on them and said, *"Receive the Holy Spirit"* (John 20:22). Why would He tell them to wait for power if they already had power? It's because they had not been entrusted with the power of the Holy Spirit yet.

They had been entrusted with the indwelling presence of the Spirit. This was a different experience of which the Lord was speaking. Since they had already been filled internally, He now wanted to clothe them externally.

"Wait and you shall receive." Who are we waiting on? Or what are we waiting on? Jesus said that the coming of the Holy Spirit upon us was the promise of the Father (see Luke 24:49). If the

Father promises something, you can bet your bottom dollar that He wants to give it to you. The key is waiting on the Lord, who is the baptizer. Jesus said that He would pray to the Father and that the Father would send the Holy Spirit (see John 14:16).

Now, just think of this for a moment. Let's look at the words of Jesus. John 14:16 says, *"And I will pray the Father, and he shall give you another Comforter, that he may abide with you for ever"* (KJV). Isn't this beautiful? Let's look at this simple spiritual equation for a moment. The coming of the Holy Spirit upon you is the promise of the Father. You have Jesus praying to the Father for you to receive the power of the Holy Spirit. When Jesus prays, the Father honors Him. *That* I can assure you.

Perhaps you've thought for a long time, "Well, maybe I just don't qualify for the power of God. Maybe I have too much sin in my life. Maybe I've messed up too much in the past." Did you know that your past means nothing to the Lord once you come to Jesus and ask Him to forgive your sin? There is not a single one of us alive today who earns the power of the Holy Spirit outside of the mercy and grace of the blood of Jesus. We have qualified for the power of the Holy Spirit because Jesus has qualified us through His sinless life, death, burial, resurrection, and ascension. It is His work that we are grafted into, receiving blessings that we don't deserve!

> *Thank You, Holy Spirit, that I don't qualify myself for Your presence or Your power. The cross is the only thing that qualifies me, so I receive the grace and blood of Jesus again today. Would You clothe me with power? I want Your power to transform me from the inside, out. I want every person who comes into contact with me to be drawn to You.*

83

Testimony

Many believe that certain gifts must manifest when somebody has had a legitimate Holy Spirit baptism. That is not my perspective, but I respect the others who believe this way. The true evidence that somebody has been empowered by the Holy Spirit is not the gift of tongues, according to Jesus. For Him, the true sign is power. Power to do what? To be a witness unto Jesus to the ends of the earth. Notice Jesus did not say that we will witness once we have received the power of the Holy Spirit. He said we will be a witness (see Acts 1:8). Your life literally becomes a testimony of who Jesus is to the entire world around you once the Holy Spirit plugs you into power from Heaven. That power dethrones and destroys the influence of the devil in people's lives.

Acts 10:38 says, *"God anointed Jesus of Nazareth with the Holy Spirit and power, and how He went around doing good and healing all who were under the power of the devil, because God was with Him."*

The power of the Holy Spirit sets people free. It is literally the power of Heaven against what binds millions of people around you today. I want to be very clear about this: Without the power of the Holy Spirit, people stay unsaved, they stay sick, they stay depressed, and fear will continue to dominate them. Sickness mocks all of us unless we are clothed with the power of the Holy Spirit. It is not a side issue. It is not a minor benefit on top of a ministry that we create. Unless our lives are flowing in the power of the Holy Spirit, we don't have a ministry.

> *Holy Spirit, thank You that You long to bring healing to people, see restoration come to families, and witness a transformed world even more than I do! Fill me completely so that every area of my life will proclaim the gospel of Jesus Christ. Let Your power flow through me so that every person will get a glimpse of Your nature.*

84

THE HEART OF GOD

"It is not by might, it is not by power, but it is by My Spirit,' says the Lord" (see Zech. 4:6). We must realize that no matter how smart and organized we feel we are, while it might look in the natural like things are happening, nothing eternal takes place outside of the power of the Holy Spirit. If Jesus needed the power of the Holy Spirit, we need it today. It's important to remember, however, that this is not a vague power. It is not a higher power. It is a power that flows from a person; that's why it's called the power of the Holy Spirit.

The mission of the Holy Spirit is to glorify Jesus. Jesus is glorified when He receives what He paid for. For example, Jesus paid for the salvation of the entire world. Every time somebody is genuinely saved, it glorifies Jesus. It says to the princes and the principalities of the air, to Heaven, and to everybody standing around on the earth that Jesus is enough to change our lives, that He is alive, and that He is still King over our sin. Every time somebody is healed, it glorifies Jesus because it brings into the here and now what the Scripture says Jesus paid for: "*...by His stripes we are healed*" (Isa. 53:5). It shows that God is faithful to His promises. When a demon is cast out, it says that God has come. As Jesus said, "When devils are cast out, it's because the Kingdom has come" (see Luke 11:20; Matt. 12:28). It reveals to the world that Jesus is greater than any power in the universe.

I do not have to beg for You to come. I do not have to plead for You to heal, set free, or restore. You are the Healer, the Restorer, the only One who brings true freedom. It is who You are. It is the heart of the Father. Holy Spirit, show me an aspect of God's heart for me that has grown dim in my thinking lately. What would You have me remember about the heart of God today?

85

The Power of the Trinity

Jesus was on a mission to reveal the Father to the world. He was the literal embodiment and perfect image of the Father. Hebrews 1 tells us that Jesus is the very *"brightness of His glory"* (Heb. 1:3). Jesus is not only the brightness of God's glory; He is the "very" brightness of His glory. He is the apex of God's highest height. He is the brightest light and the crescendo of God. So, to look at Him is to see absolute holy perfection. He is the Word of God. The Bible says, *"The Word became flesh and dwelt among us…"* (John 1:14).

The Bible also tells us in Hebrews 1, *"In these last days* [God has] *spoken to us by His Son…"* (Heb. 1:2) Another way to think of this is to say, "He has spoken His Son to us." So, what is the Father saying? It's really simple. He is always saying, "JESUS." It is His only message and sermon. The Scriptures tells us clearly: He was *"in the bosom of the Father"* (John 1:18). Jesus literally is the heartbeat of our loving Father. To see Jesus is to see the heart of the Father. To receive Jesus is to receive the Father's heart and only sermon.

> *I never need to be confused about God's heart for me. I never need to doubt His intentions for those I love. He has shown me beyond a shadow of a doubt through His Son, Jesus. Holy Spirit, thank You for dwelling in me, an imperfect being. Thank You for empowering Heaven to invade earth. Thank You for every instance where You've conquered death and destruction, releasing Your life-giving power over us.*

86

Clothed with the Spirit

Jesus told His disciples to "wait in Jerusalem until you are empowered from on high" (see Luke 24:49). Why would He instruct us to wait for the Holy Spirit? Because without His power, we don't have a chance of revealing Jesus. With His power, revealing Jesus is natural and normal.

I've personally prayed for tens of thousands of people since 1989. I have seen more and greater miracles than I ever thought I would. Early on in my ministry, the Lord began to teach me something loud and clear: The devil doesn't recognize who I am friends with. He doesn't care if I'm part of a big church or a small church. He is not going to leave someone I am praying for because of the size of my social media following. Neither does he care if I have famous friends and family. This one may ruffle some feathers—but he doesn't care about the length of time I have been saved. Only two things are of issue when praying for the sick and oppressed: whose you are and who is on you.

Let me make it plain and simple, and maybe a little old school: Is there Holy Ghost power flowing through your being? You can't say, "In the name of my church, be healed." You can't say, "In the name of my favorite preacher, be healed." This is what matters: the name of Jesus in the power of the Holy Spirit. The enemy knows if you've been touched by the Holy Spirit. He has a good eye for finding those who are clothed with the Spirit. Why? Because he's afraid of the One who clothes us. He runs from Him. He hates the Holy Spirit and His power because he knows his grip on people's lives is destroyed when he bumps into heavenly power. Remember what the Bible says: "It is the anointing that destroys the yoke" (see Isa. 10:27).

Dear Lord, the enemy cowers at Your Spirit. I don't have to promote myself to know that the One in me breaks every chain of bondage. Holy Spirit, flow through me.

87

Honoring God's Friends

I'm completely blown away by the grace of God. As I look back at my life and our ministry, it's impossible not to see the fingerprints of those who paid a dear price so that I could walk in a deeper measure of God. First of all, I owe the Lord everything, but I also owe His friends so much. There is an inheritance in the Holy Spirit. I truly believe that this generation is to walk in a greater measure of the Holy Spirit than the generation before us. When I think of the breakthrough in the lives of the champions of the generation before mine, I am blown away by the mark they have set. We have a lot of work to do, friends. Yet in the Lord, everything is possible.

I believe a greater flow of the Holy Spirit is going to hit the world and the Church than we've ever seen in our lives. But as we step into this and seek God, let's never forget those who have touched our lives.

Maybe it would make me look more self-sufficient if I looked at you and said that everything I have experienced in the Lord came through a sovereign encounter while being alone with Him, but that's just not the case. If you trace church history, it's never been the case. If you look back at your life, I'm sure you can trace most encounters with God to the cooperation of one of God's friends. That combination impacted you, and I pray that will be said of us in the years to come—that you and I were used to impact others in the Holy Spirit. I am so grateful for all those who have paid a price so that I could know the Lord more deeply.

According to Jesus, when we receive His friends, we receive Him, and when we receive Him, we receive the Father who sent Him (see Matt. 10:40). To receive God's friends is to receive God Himself.

Holy Spirit, You are drawn to the atmosphere of honor. And You have placed leaders and mentors so strategically in my life to teach, guide, and model a life in pursuit of You. Will You bring to mind some of the individuals that went before me—whether I know them personally or not—who deserve my honor? What aspect of Your heart did these people reveal to me?

88

EVERY GOOD GIFT

As I look back on my life with the Holy Spirit, it is absolutely crystal clear to me that I am a recipient of what God gave to others before me. I have been impacted by so many amazing people who knew the Lord deeply. My parents, Theo and Evelyn Koulianos, fought for my soul during my teen years. My parents are so selfless and faithful. Beyond a shadow of a doubt, my father-in-law, Benny Hinn, has had a great spiritual impact on my life. How could I ever repay them? It's safe to say that there would be no Jesus Image and that I would not be in the ministry, born again, or healthy had God not raised up Benny. Not to mention he let me marry his daughter thirteen years ago. That's not a bad deal.

So much of what is taking place in Jesus Image and in my life personally is due to an unquestionable impartation that has occurred over the last twenty-seven years. It is amazing to think that God can take what He has given me and what He has given you and share it with others.

The Greek word for *impartation* is *metadidómi.* It means "to give over, to share, to give, to impart." It can also mean "to give a share of." It can mean "to communicate, to relate, to give, or to bestow." It can also mean "to transmit, pass on, or confer, and transfer."

It's important we understand that while God will use men and women as instruments of impartation, all that we receive comes from the Lord. The Bible says it is *"of His fullness we have all received…"* (John 1:16). Again, Jesus told the disciples, *"…[Wait] in the city of Jerusalem until you are endued with power from on high"* (Luke 24:49). That Scripture highlights so much, but the portion that I believe we often miss is this: that the power must come from on high.

The power must come from on high because that's where Jesus is. He is the baptizer of the Holy Spirit. Every good gift comes down from above (see James 1:17). We can never take credit or give man the credit for what flows from God alone. While we should honor, we must forever remember the source: Jesus Himself.

Your generosity is overwhelming, Holy Spirit. You long to bestow Your love, grace, mercy and power upon me. Thank You for your servants who have taught me truth, showed me love, and imparted Your power to me. You are the giver of every good thing in my life. I am forever grateful for You.

89

IN AND UPON

When the apostles back in Jerusalem heard that the people of Samaria had accepted God's message, they sent Peter and John there. As soon as they arrived, they prayed for these new believers to receive the Holy Spirit. The Holy Spirit had not yet come upon any of them, for they had only been baptized in the name of the Lord Jesus. Then Peter and John laid their hands upon these believers, and they received the Holy Spirit (Acts 8:14-17 NLT).

What a beautiful picture of the Holy Spirit's work in us! Remember when Jesus breathed on the disciples in John 20 and said, *"Receive the Holy Spirit"*. It was also the moment that the Holy Spirit began to live on the inside of them and filled their spirits. They became the temple of the Holy Spirit. This is called the indwelling of the Holy Spirit, the presence of God within us. Every born-again Christian is filled with the Holy Spirit. I am talking about something entirely different. I am referring to what Jesus was talking about in Acts 1:8 when He said, "*Ye shall receive power, after that the Holy Spirit is come upon you*" (KJV). The moment He comes upon us, power is ours, and that is what I am talking about right now.

These Samaritan believers had already received Jesus as the indwelling Lord, by the Holy Spirit, but they had yet to be empowered for ministry service. The Holy Spirit within us connects us with the Lord and gives us the opportunity to fellowship with Jesus at any time and any place. He is a fountain of living water on the inside, no matter where we go. But the Holy Spirit on us empowers us to break the power of the devil off of those who desperately need Jesus. The Bible says, "It is the anointing (or the smearing of power) that destroys the yoke" (see Isa. 10:27).

Thank You, Holy Spirit, that the very moment I gave my life to Jesus, You took up residence in my heart. Thank You that, from that very moment, You have been transforming me from the inside to look more like Jesus every day. But I need more of You. I need to receive Your power. I need You to rest upon me so that You can show the world who You are.

90

The Laying on of Hands

Ananias went his way, and entered into the house; and putting his hands on him said, Brother Saul, the Lord, even Jesus, that appeared unto thee in the way as thou camest, hath sent me, that thou mightest receive thy sight, and be filled with the Holy Ghost. And immediately there fell from his eyes as it had been scales: and he received sight forthwith, and arose, and was baptized.... And straightway he preached Christ in the synagogues, that he is the Son of God (Acts 9:17–18,20 KJV).

As a result of Ananias laying hands on Saul, there was absolutely a transfer of the power of the Holy Spirit in Saul's life. We would call this the baptism of the Holy Spirit. Remember, Saul came to the Lord on the road to Damascus, but he was not ready to preach the Gospel in the way that Jesus did without having the same power that Jesus had. Notice it was after Ananias laid hands on Paul and he received the power of the Holy Spirit that *"he preached Christ in the synagogues, that He is the Son of God"* (Acts 9:20). Was Ananias the source? No, he was the channel of Jesus the baptizer.

In Ephesus, the apostle Paul did exactly what Ananias did to him. Acts 19:6 says, *"And when Paul laid his hands upon them, the Holy Ghost came on them; and they spake with tongues, and prophesied"* (KJV). These believers were released in a completely new world in the Holy Spirit, receiving the gift of prophecy and the ability to speak with new tongues. The gifts of the Holy Spirit can also be transferred through impartation and the laying on of hands. The apostle Paul said to his son in the faith, Timothy, *"Neglect not the gift that is in thee, which was given thee by prophecy, with the laying on of hands of the* [elders]. *Meditate upon these things; give thyself wholly to them; that thy profiting may appear to all"* (1 Tim. 4:14–15 KJV). This is impartation. The gifts that Paul and the elders carried were imparted to Timothy. In Second Timothy 1:6, Paul reminds Timothy again, *"Wherefore I put thee in remembrance that thou stir up the gift of God, which is in thee by the putting on of my hands"* (KJV).

In Acts 6, the Bible says, *"...and when they prayed, they laid their hands on them. And the Word of God increased..."* (Acts 6:6–7 KJV). This laying on of hands produced great power in the life of Stephen. The Bible says, *"Stephen, full of faith and power, did great wonders and miracles among the people"* (Acts 6:8 KJV). The Greek word for *power* is *dunamis*. It means "natural capability, power, capability to do anything, ability to perform anything, absolutely nothing is impossible, complete power and action." Something happened in the life of Stephen when the apostles laid hands on him.

You never meant for me to be an island, Holy Spirit. I was never designed to only walk with You and no one else. I was also designed to live in community with other believers. You created me to both give and receive from my brothers and sisters in Christ. Holy Spirit, will You show me right now if there is anything in my heart hindering my fellowship with Your Body?

91

SPIRITUAL CREDIBILITY

Moses said to the Lord, "May the Lord, the God who gives breath to all living things, appoint someone over this community to go and come in before them, one who will lead them out and bring them in, so the Lord's people will not be like sheep without a shepherd." So, the Lord said to Moses, "Take Joshua, son of Nun, a man in whom is the spirit of leadership, and lay your hand on him. Have him stand before Eleazar the priest and the entire assembly and commission him in their presence. Give him some of your authority so the whole Israelite community will obey him. He is to stand before Eleazar the priest, who will obtain decisions for him by inquiring of the Urim before the Lord. At his command, he and the entire community of the Israelites will go out he and at his command they will come in." Moses did as the Lord commanded him. He took Joshua, and had him stand before Eleazar the priest and the whole assembly. Then he laid

> *his hands on him and commissioned him, as the Lord instructed through Moses* (Numbers 27:15–23 NIV).

Notice Moses imparted honor and authority. Those Hebrew words mean "beauty, brilliance, grandeur, excellence, glory, honor." This impartation gave Joshua a spiritual credibility to which the people responded. In Deuteronomy 34, we see that Joshua received an impartation of wisdom from the hands of Moses. It says in verse 9: *"Joshua the son of Nun was full of the Spirit of wisdom; for Moses had laid his hands upon him: and the children of Israel hearkened unto him, and did as the Lord commanded Moses"* (Deut. 34:9 KJV). Just think, Joshua left with heavenly wisdom after God's servant prayed for him.

> *I want to sit with You right now, Holy Spirit, and think of all of the people who have poured into me. Will You bring to mind the qualities, strengths, and graces that have been imparted to me by others? I know that I wouldn't be the same without the leaders in my life. How would You have me honor those individuals today?*

92

IMPARTATION OF POWER

If you trace revival history and study the lives of those who have shaken the world, all of them had been impacted by those who went before them and by those who lived among them. Reinhard Bonnke is a dear friend of mine and somebody whom I look up to so much. You'd have to search the world through to find a man like Reinhard. Many times, over a meal, or over a private time of fellowship, Reinhard shares the stories of when George Jeffreys, the great English revivalist, laid hands on him. Reinhard left that place completely changed—"full of the glory of God," Reinhard said.

I have spoken to those who have told me that Aimee Semple McPherson was used in the life of Kathryn Kuhlman. F. F. Bosworth helped Maria Woodworth-Etter in her meetings. Lester Sumrall was deeply impacted by the life of Smith Wigglesworth. Benny

Hinn was touched by the life of Kathryn Kuhlman. Bill Johnson was deeply impacted by John Wimber and the Toronto Blessing. Steve Hill was touched by the Argentine Revival and the ministry of Pastor Benny. Heidi Baker was changed in the revival meeting in Toronto. The point is this: While everything comes from the Lord, the Lord has decided to use His friends to give away what God has given them.

While I cannot give you everything I have, I can pray and ask that an impartation will live in this book and that impartation of the power of the Holy Spirit will come on you now and change your life. This is what I am believing for you: number one, that through this impartation, the presence of God would be more real to you than ever; number two, that an anointing to pray and spend time with Jesus would be yours; number three, that the love of God would flow in you and through you; number four, that you would break the power of the devil off of people's lives, and that mighty miracles, signs, and wonders would flow through you; number five, that the declaration of the Gospel would come out of your mouth like fire; and number six, that all of your family and friends would receive what you're about to receive right now.

Heavenly Father, I come to You needy; I need You, Lord. You said that I could ask You for anything in the name of Jesus, and so I come, asking for an impartation. Holy Spirit, I need You. Jesus, I receive the power, the favor, the wisdom, and every gift of the Holy Spirit that You have for me now.

93

HIS BREATH, HIS VOICE

The angel of the Lord appeared to him in a blazing fire from the midst of a bush; and he looked, and behold, the bush was burning with fire, yet the bush was not consumed. So Moses said, "I must turn aside now and see this marvelous sight, why the bush is not burned up." When the Lord saw that he turned aside to look, God called to him from the midst of the bush and said, "Moses, Moses!" And he said, "Here I am." Then He said, "Do not come near here; remove your sandals from your feet, for the place on which you are standing is holy ground." He said also, "I am the God of your father, the God of Abraham, the God of Isaac, and the God of Jacob." Then Moses hid his face, for he was afraid to look at God (Exodus 3:2–6 NASB).

Notice in verse 4 that the voice of the Lord came from the midst of the bush (see Exod. 3:4). When you combine that truth with the words of Jesus in John 6, "My words are spirit...," we experience a beautiful revelation (see John 6:63). His voice flows from Him and is full of Him. Think of it this way: To hear God, I must come to God, and His voice is wrapped in His Spirit.

Once you discover this, you'll never read the Scriptures the same way again! You won't come to your Bible anymore. You will come to Jesus through your Bible. You'll begin to look at every verse as a living moment in the Holy Spirit. The Bible was never meant to be merely read. Rather, it was intended to be seen, heard, felt, meditated on, and eaten. When you sit down and invite the Holy Spirit to teach you and lead you as you read the Scriptures, you will begin to experience His breath, which is His voice.

I come to Your Word, feeling aware that I am standing on holy ground. I come to Your Word ready to encounter You, Holy Spirit. You have infused Your presence into Your holy Scriptures, and I refuse to think of reading my Bible as anything but a life-giving encounter with You. Show me where in Your Word You would have me read today. I come filled with expectancy.

94

His Heart on Display

Have you ever tried to speak without breathing? Unless there is the release of breath, we cannot make a sound. When God speaks in His Word, He releases His breath, the Holy Spirit!

The Bible says it is *"out of the abundance of the heart* [that] *the mouth speaks"* (Matt. 12:34). This is amazing. Remember, even though Jesus said this to others, it also reveals to us how He works. More specifically, it gives us a beautiful picture of His internal workings. So, think of this for a moment: whatever Jesus says is the revelation of His heart. I like to say it this way: "The Bible is God's heart on paper." Unlike us at times, Jesus doesn't "just say things" and not mean what He says. He is pure truth. That means that His heart is on full display in the Word. What a privilege to see Him this way!

To love the Word of God is to love God's voice, which is Spirit.

To love the Word of God is to love His face, from which the voice flows.

To love the Word of God is to love God's breath, which is the Holy Spirit Himself.

To love the Word of God is to love His heart.

The other side of the coin is:

To not love the Word is to not love the voice of God, which is Spirit.

To not love the Spirit is to not love His face, from which the voice flows.

To not love the Word is to not love the breath of God, which is the Holy Spirit.

To not love the Word is to not love His heart.

As you read the pure truth of the Scriptures, I believe your heart and mind will open into a fresh revelation of the beauty and power of the Spirit.

What a privilege it is to have access to Your Scriptures! What a joy it is to see Your heart evident on the pages. How beautiful it is that I get to encounter Your very heartbeat through Your Word. Forgive me, Holy Spirit, for any time that I have forgotten the value of Your Word. Help me to experience the Bible as the treasure that it truly is.

95

Constant and Faithful

When the Holy Spirit becomes your friend and a conversation begins between you and Him, He will literally blow your mind. You will discover that He never stops working, He never stops speaking. He is constantly inviting us to be with Him. He loves to nudge us and ask us to do something to reveal the love of Jesus in the lives of others. I have found that He has an incredible sense of humor, and He will also shock us at times.

One thing I'm learning as I walk with Him more closely is that He does not compartmentalize our lives. I believe the day of ministers touching people's lives on the platform alone are coming to an end. The Holy Spirit does not have an off switch, and He does not turn off when we leave a pulpit or a platform. His heart still burns for people. I would venture to say that the coming wave of evangelism that will sweep the nations of the earth will not be dominated by public ministry but by everyday people like you and me who are simply listening to the Holy Spirit as we get close to Him and obey Him.

It's important we understand that life in the Holy Spirit is not a concept but a life. He's not a topic, but a person. He's not a subject, but an individual who longs to live with us, and among us, and in us.

Life with the Holy Spirit might be many things, but I can assure you that it is far from boring. Yes, He will challenge you. Yes, He will take you to the end of yourself with His spoken word, wanting you to obey. But He always has something up His sleeve that we can't see. He always has something better than we can ever imagine waiting for us on the other end. The Scripture says, "No eye has seen, no ear has heard, no mind conceived what God has in store for those who love Him" (see 1 Cor. 2:9).

Holy Spirit, I invite You wholeheartedly into every area of my life. I don't want to shut You out of any aspect of my day. I want to walk with You through every moment, pulling on Your wisdom, seeing from Your perspective, and hearing Your voice. Challenge me today, Holy Spirit. Help me to grow in my awareness of and trust in You.

96

Today Is Your Day

Out of the corner of my eye, across the parking lot of a gas station in a horrible neighborhood I saw a man walking with a shopping cart. He was clearly homeless and walked with a noticeable limp. The moment he caught my eye, I heard the Holy Spirit say, "Go and lay hands on him and pray for his ailment."

So, I left the gas nozzle in my car and immediately left my car unattended and walked over to the man who clearly had a very, very injured leg. Once I introduced myself, he gave me his name, which I'll never forget. It was Jack. Initially, he was very scared. He thought I was going to hurt him. As I talked to him about Jesus, I put my hand on the man's hip, right there in the middle of the parking lot. As I did that, I felt something on me. Now I know it was the presence of the Spirit. I took his shopping cart and pushed it away from him. He panicked.

He said, "You don't understand—I can't walk without that cart." The man was so poor he did not have money for a walker or a cane, so that cart had become his personal mobility assistance device. Led of the Spirit, I took the cart and pushed it away from him. Now he had no cart at all. He said, "I can't walk without it."

I said, "Well, you're going to have to. Today is your day." I grabbed his hand and began to walk with him through the parking lot. And after the first few steps, I saw a tear running down his face.

He said, "You don't understand—I couldn't do this before." And then he started to walk more, and more, and more, and more, until his pace increased and the Lord had touched and healed him. His eyes were full of tears, and they streamed down his face. I'll never forget that day, not because it was the greatest miracle I've ever seen. It sticks out to me because of the way that the Holy Spirit orchestrated the whole thing. The last place I thought I'd see miracles is at the gas pump, but the beauty of the will of the Spirit is like nothing we've ever known.

Thank You, Holy Spirit, that You know how to guide me. I have tuned my ear to Your voice. I have invited Your interruption into every moment of my life. I want to be used by You, and You know exactly how to get my attention. Give me boldness, Holy Spirit. Help me to leave behind any vestige of fear or control. I want to see Your name glorified on the earth!

97

The Master Healer

A friend of mine named Dave Popovici, who is now a missionary in northern Iraq, invited me to preach at his church in Chicago. When I went to the church, I began to teach on the presence of Jesus. I could sense the power of God as I was speaking. The people were hungry; they were gripped. When I was through preaching, as I usually do, I went back into worship. As we began to worship the Lord, I felt His power come upon me. There is no denying the power of the Holy Spirit when it begins to flow. Sometimes I feel tingling all over my body. Sometimes I feel electricity flowing through my hands. Sometimes my hands feel like they each weigh twenty pounds. Sometimes my entire body is flooded with life and joy.

A young girl grabbed my attention. She was standing there with her mother, and she was about five years old at the time. I noticed she had huge Coke-bottle glasses on. She was a precious little girl with a very sweet spirit. I walked up to her, took off her glasses, and I prayed for her eyes. The power of God hit her, and I walked away to pray for others. It was an awesome meeting, but I never got a testimony from the little girl or her mother.

Five years later, I was preaching across the country near Sacramento, California, in a conference that our friend was hosting. As I began to minister, that same power began to flow again. This time, people were healed of multiple issues, and they began to fall under the power of God. It really was a glorious meeting. I noticed a young mother with a daughter who seemed to be twelve or thirteen years old. They walked up to me, but while they looked a bit familiar, I could not place their faces.

The mother said, "I have a testimony to share with you and this whole church." So, I gave her the microphone. She said, "Five years ago, Michael came to my church in Chicago. He walked up to my daughter, put his hand on her, and prayed that God would give her vision back. The power of God swept through my daughter, and that night her eyes were completely healed. In fact, when she put her Coke-bottle glasses on, everything was blurry and she could not see. I just want to share this testimony with all of you so that you can see what God did in that meeting with Michael."

I'm the first to realize that I do not deserve to see these things. When I do see them, I am in awe of God. The lady continued to share the testimony of her daughter—that she had been completely healed and made whole and that since that day, she had begun to encounter God in a beautiful way. The Holy Spirit is the master healer, and you can trust Him to use your life in the same way.

All healing comes from You, Holy Spirit. So, right now, I lift up the people in my life who need to experience Your healing presence. Would You wash over them like You did that little girl? Every sickness, pain, and disease must bow its knee to the name of Jesus. Holy Spirit, fill me up so that I might pour Your presence out on the people who are hurting around me.

98

Celebrating the Risk

Our family loves to visit Winter Park, Florida. It's about twenty minutes from our home. It's a beautiful downtown district with cobblestone streets and stunning aged oak trees. The buildings are classical. The shopping is great, and so is the food. One day, we went down to Winter Park with our family to have some lunch and get the kids dessert. They love ice cream. When we were through at the ice cream shop, I walked outside the store and looked to my left. There was an elderly woman sitting on a bench. I grabbed my kids and said, "Guys, come watch this."

You see, I want my children to know how simple it is to walk with the Holy Spirit and how He brings the love of Jesus much more clearly and beautifully than we ever could in our own strength. I also want them to see the fruit of obedience. Some of us believe that if we don't see the miracle, we failed. No, we have to teach our children to celebrate taking risks. So, I walked up to this woman, sat down on the bench next to her with my children and my brother-in-law Josh, and I said, "Ma'am, my name is Michael. I'm a minister here in the area. The Lord sent me to you."

She said, "Really?"

I said, "Yes, He did. Do you have any pain in your body?"

"I do, actually," she replied.

I asked, "Do you mind if I lay hands on you and pray for you?"

She said, "No, I don't mind. Please do."

So, I put my hand on her, and I told my children, "Guys, come over here. You pray for her too." And so, they began to pray for this dear woman, and she became very emotional. I said, "Ma'am, has the pain left your body?"

"It has! It has!" She exclaimed, "Who are you?"

I just said, "Just somebody who is following Jesus." My kids were blown away that God would use them in that way. I remember my brother-in-law asking, "Dude, does that happen everywhere you go?" How I wish it did! But it is happening more and more and more as I learn to listen to and obey the voice of the Holy Spirit.

I want to be like a child in Your presence, Holy Spirit. I want to sit at Your feet in expectation, full of trust in You. Purify my heart, Holy Spirit. Strip away anything that has become hardened with disappointment or shame. Fill me with Your love, heal me and transform me. I surrender it all to You, again and again. I am Yours.

99

He Empowers the Obedient

One evening, we were in a large crusade with my father-in-law. In those days, I would learn the voice of the Spirit by walking through the crowd and asking Him who He was healing. I learned it was more effective to join what God was doing and agree with the people He was already touching in the crowd. That is not the only way to see miracles, but since we were under a time restraint, the Holy Spirit began to show me this way of seeing breakthrough for those who are suffering. As I walked through the crowd, I noticed that my wife was speaking to a lady. There were people gathered around her in a huge circle, not to mention an entire section of people above her looking down. It was quite a scene. Jessica saw me and called me over to her.

She said, "My husband can pray." And I thought to myself, *What? What kind of pressure is this? Besides, I'm not the healer. I can't open any ears on my best day.* Well, I knew what Jess meant, but it still put a lot of pressure on me and at the time was something for which I was not ready. There was a huge crowd standing around us in a circle with a deaf person standing in the middle. Beyond that, as I said, an entire section of the church was above us looking down. I prayed for the woman. I put my finger in her ear and commanded her ears to open. I was very nervous. Nothing happened when I prayed.

I asked, "Can you hear?"

"No," she replied.

I tried again. Nothing happened. At this point, I was so embarrassed. Here I was, called out and in a stadium with people watching. I'm in the ministry, and I can't get these ears to open. So, I tried again—nothing happened. For some reason, something deep in my soul said, "Just don't give up. Keep going." I tried a fourth time. I said, "Ma'am, can you hear?"

"No," she said.

I tried a fifth time. "Open, in Jesus' name!" Nothing. A sixth time—nothing happened. It was the seventh time, I believe, that I just stayed with it and said, "In Jesus' name, open!"

I will never forget the look on this woman's face when my mouth uttered the word "open." Her eyes got huge. The smile was all consuming. Excitement was beaming out of her face, and she began to scream, "They're open! I can hear! I can hear!"

Can you imagine the first thing you would hear in a stadium full of people worshiping Jesus? Well, I was as emotional as she was. For the life of me, I couldn't believe it. What a lesson the Holy Spirit taught me—that He empowers us when we step out. He empowers those who take risks. He energizes the moments of those who put their reputations aside and are willing to look foolish for His glory.

> *Holy Spirit, thank You that You never turn Your back on me, even when my faith is low or I'm filled with fear. I will trade my reputation gladly if it means I get more of You. Holy Spirit, I want to move with You today. What would You have me do for Your glory?*

100

PERMISSION

One evening, in Baldwin Park, Florida, where my brother Theo was pastoring at the time, I was asked to lead a Bible study in a very young church plant that he and his wife, Rachel, were orchestrating. It was a very small group of maybe eight people. We sat in a circle with our Bibles open, and I began to teach the Scriptures. A woman walked in off the street. It was pretty clear that she did not know the Lord and she was searching for help.

She came in and said, "I just left the ER, where my daughter is because she tried to kill herself by taking pills. She did not die, but she almost did." It was clear that the mother was very distraught and sad. So, she came seeking help and peace. As she began to share the horrific details of what she and her daughter were going through, she also shared with me that her husband had left her. Now she was all alone with a daughter trying to commit suicide. She was on her way back to her house, which was just across the street from where we were hosting the Bible study, and she decided to come in.

The woman began to share her pain. She looked at me and said, "I have this huge goiter—this growth on my neck. Do you think God could heal it? Would you pray for me?" Very simply, by faith, I felt the presence of the Holy Spirit, and I put my hand on her neck. I would say it was about the size of a tangerine. Until the day I die, I will never forget what I felt under my hand when we simply obeyed the Holy Spirit and spoke the name of Jesus. I felt a pop, and I felt something under my hand change. It was like something disappeared. When I looked for the growth again, it was completely gone. I was blown away—so was she, and so were the people sitting around us. She began to touch her neck over and over again. "Where is it? Oh my gosh, it's gone. Where is it? Where is it? Where is it? It's gone!" We all began to celebrate God's goodness, and I'll never forget driving home that night. I saw her walking to her house, and she was still feeling for the growth that was gone.

I want to challenge you today: Give God permission to shock you. Give God permission to mess up your schedule. Between point A and point B today, give God permission to ask you to stop for somebody. When He speaks, simply obey like a little child, and remember that you're not the healer; Jesus is. God is not looking for you to work a great miracle. He simply is looking for you to obey Him and to leave the rest to Him. I hope you'll enjoy the Holy Spirit today like you never have before.

Holy Spirit, I open up my heart, my body, my entire life to Your presence. I give You permission to shock me. I give You permission to slow me down, to interrupt my plans, and to interrupt my schedule. I trust You completely. I am in awe of all that I am learning of You. Fill me with Your presence and flow through me, Holy Spirit. I will go wherever You send me and do whatever You ask of me. You are the delight of my life.

About Michael Koulianos

Michael Koulianos is the founder of Jesus Image, an international ministry consisting of three parts: Jesus Image Church, a family of believers in Orlando who burn for the presence of Jesus Himself; Jesus School, a ministry school with a mission to raise up a company of Jesus People; and Jesus Events, nationwide events where thousands gather to worship and encounter God. He has also authored several books, including *The Jesus Book: Fall Recklessly in Love with Jesus*, *Holy Spirit: The One Who Makes Jesus Real*, *Jesus 365: A Daily Devotional with the Son of God*, and *Healing Presence: Discover the Healing Power of the Word of God.*

From

CHAZDON STRICKLAND

Learn to walk in the supernatural realities you've seen in the Bible!

Jesus wants to teach you how to live a supernatural life! When He walked the Earth, Jesus trained His disciples to walk in the miraculous by healing the sick, casting out demons, raising the dead, and bringing the Kingdom of Heaven to Earth. This is Jesus' definition of "normal life."

Today, we need a supernatural upgrade to bring us back to Jesus' vision for what is normal.

Chazdon Strickland is a pastor and trainer. He recognizes his assignment is not to simply build a congregation, but to train every believer on how to enter, access, and release the glory of God based on Jesus' model.

The Old Testament prophets saw a day when the knowledge of God's glory would flood the Earth. Today is that day! Get ready to walk in the supernatural realms and realities you've read about in Scripture!

Purchase your copy wherever books are sold

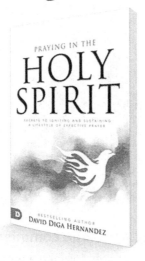

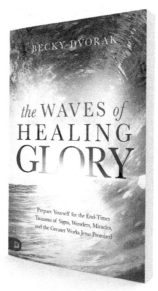

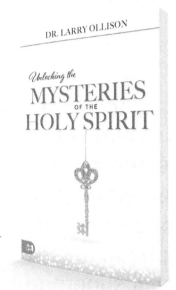

From

Corey Russell

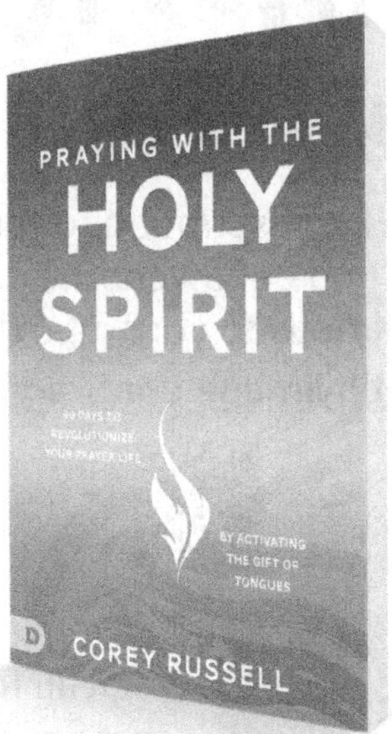

Unlock Realms of Glory through Praying in Tongues!

Is your vision of praying in tongues too small? Is it unbiblical?

Too often we, as believers, avoid praying in tongues due to confusion or misunderstanding. Yet we've unknowingly laid aside one of the most powerful tools in our spiritual arsenal. This gift brings us out of the flesh and into the Spirit—enabling us to pray from a position of victory, rout the spiritual forces of darkness, and experience a richer relationship with the Lord.

In *Praying with the Holy Spirit,* Corey Russell, a key intercessor and leader, shows you how to activate this supernatural gift, opening up new depths of intimacy with God and igniting you to pray with unshakable fervency, authority, and confidence against any enemy scheme.

Based on his bestselling book *The Glory Within*, this 40-day guided devotional journal takes you on a life-changing journey into the heart of what it means to pray in tongues—and how to do it effectively.

Don't settle for a powerless prayer life. It's time to engage the Spirit, unlock new realms of glory, and unleash the supernatural power of praying in tongues in your world.

Purchase your copy wherever books are sold